A St. John the Divine Life Group Study

The Disciple's Way

JOURNEYING WITH JESUS TO JERUSALEM

WRITTEN BY

THE REV. CHARLIE HOLT, THE REV. LOUISE SAMUELSON,
THE REV. REAGAN COCKE, THE REV. GREG BUFFONE,
THE RT. REV. GARY LILLIBRIDGE

The Disciple's Way

JOURNEYING WITH JESUS TO JERUSALEM

WRITTEN BY

THE REV. CHARLIE HOLT, THE REV. LOUISE SAMUELSON,
THE REV. REAGAN COCKE, THE REV. GREG BUFFONE,
THE RT. REV. GARY LILLIBRIDGE

EDITED BY GINNY MOONEY

The Disciple's Way: Journeying to Jerusalem with Jesus

© 2019 The Church of St. John the Divine

All rights reserved.

Published in Houston, Texas by Bible Study Media, Inc.

Design by Docent Research Group.

ISBN # 978-1-942243-27-4

Library of Congress Control Number: 2019913494

No part of this publication may be reproduced, stored in retrieval system, or transmitted in any form or by any means electronic, mechanical, photocopy, recording, or otherwise except for brief quotations in printed reviews, without the prior written permission of the publisher. www.biblestudymedia.com.

Unless otherwise indicated, all Scripture quotations are from the ESV® Bible (The Holy Bible, English StandardVersion®), copyright © 2001 by Crossway, a publishing ministry of Good News Publishers. Used by permission. All rights reserved.

Printed in the United States of America

THANK YOU

There are so many people who have helped make this study possible through generous donations of their time, passion, and participation. Thank you to all who have contributed to this project offered to the glory of God.

— *The Church of St. John the Divine, Houston, Texas*

Table of Contents

Introduction **8**

Week One: Blessed Eyes **12**
Week Two: True Heart **36**
Week Three: Realistic Faith **58**
Week Four: Eternal Fellowship **82**
Week Five: Generous Service **104**
Week Six: Selfless Humility **128**

The Study Guide **154**
Outline of Sessions **156**

Session 1: Blessed Eyes **160**
Session 2: True Heart **166**
Session 3: Realistic Faith **172**
Session 4: Eternal Fellowship **178**
Session 5: Generous Service **184**
Session 6: Selfless Humility **190**

Appendices

- Frequently Asked Questions **196**
- Small Group Covenant **200**
- Group Calendar **202**
- Prayer & Praise Journal **203**
- Small Group Roster **204**

Small Group Leader Helps **205**

Introduction

THE CALL OF THE DISCIPLE / READ: LUKE 9:18-27

Our story begins in *media res,* which means "in the middle of things."

The first half of the Gospel of Luke is all about figuring out the identity of Jesus. Who is this man? Where did he come from? He speaks with such authority! He has such power! Even the wind and the waves obey him.

Opinions differ as to Jesus' identity, even amongst his followers. But we come to a turning point in the ninth chapter of Luke when, in an intimate exchange, the disciples finally confess that Jesus is the Messiah, the Christ of God. From this point forward, Luke's story is not about figuring out who Jesus is, but what he came to do—and, *what his followers are called to do.*

This is where our story begins, in the middle of Luke's Gospel.

The ninth chapter launches us into what is called Luke's "travel narrative." Throughout the next ten chapters (Luke 9-19) we follow Jesus and his disciples from Galilee to Jerusalem. Their journey begins specifically in Luke 9:51 which says, *"When the days drew near for [Jesus] to be taken up, he set his face to go to Jerusalem."* The travel narrative ends just before the triumphal entry of Jesus into Jerusalem: *"And when he said these things, he went on ahead, going up to Jerusalem"* (Luke 19:28).

A travel narrative is not unique to the Gospel of Luke. In the Old Testament book of Exodus, we find the great travel narrative of the Israelites moving from bondage in Egypt to Sabbath rest in the Promised Land of Canaan. Luke's travel narrative of Jesus and his disciples takes us from Galilee in the northern part of Israel to Jerusalem in the south—a far shorter distance and briefer span of time than the exodus. Yet, like the exodus journey, Luke's narrative has far more significance than a mere shift in geography. It is the story of a *sovereign summons to a journey of life*—a life surrendered to the will of God through faith in and obedience to his Son, Jesus. It is a call to The Disciple's Way.

THE CHRIST OF GOD

Have you wrestled with the identity of Jesus as his disciples did? Who do you believe Jesus is? A great moral teacher, a wise sage, or a prophet? Or do you believe he is more than that? What do you say? As he asked his first disciples, Jesus is asking you and me, *"But who do you say that I am?"* The answer he would have us give is found on the lips of Peter in Luke 9:20: *"The Christ of God."*

Christ means Anointed One, the Messiah. Peter's confession correctly identifies Jesus as this long-awaited Messiah who is not just the hope of Israel, but the light of every tribe, every people, and every nation who believe in him. As God promised Abraham, a redeemer would come through the Jews would bless the whole world. Jesus comes to save all who would believe.

Peter does more than correctly identify Jesus as the Messiah; he identifies himself with this Messiah. He becomes a resolute follower of the Anointed One. The real challenge for Peter and the other disciples who have decided to follow begins *now*. Where is the Christ of God leading them?

> *"The Son of Man must suffer many things and be rejected by the elders and chief priests and scribes, and be killed, and on the third day be raised."* Luke 9:22

The answer is, he is leading them to Jerusalem—to the Cross and to Resurrection.

THE INVITATION

It is one thing to correctly know who Jesus is, even to believe in him; it is quite another to follow him wherever he goes. Herein lies the invitation of our study in Luke—*to truly become a disciple of Jesus.*

What does it mean to be a disciple of Jesus, the Christ of God? Jesus spells it out, *"If anyone would come after me, let him deny himself and take up his cross daily and follow me. For whoever would save his life will lose it, but whoever loses his life for my sake will save it"* (9:23-24).

The paradox of the invitation to be a disciple of Jesus is that *the path to life is a path through death.* What exactly does this mean? We'll explore the answer together in the next several weeks as we consider how to respond to Jesus' invitation. Will we decide to follow him along The Disciple's Way?

Week One

BLESSED EYES

And he said to all, "If anyone would come after me, let him deny himself and take up his cross daily and follow me. For whoever would save his life will lose it, but whoever loses his life for my sake will save it. For what does it profit a man if he gains the whole world and loses or forfeits himself? For whoever is ashamed of me and of my words, of him will the Son of Man be ashamed when he comes in his glory and the glory of the Father and of the holy angels."

LUKE 9:23-26

CONSIDER

Do you see the people of the world with the eyes of Jesus?

Day 1

SET YOUR FACE / READ LUKE 9:51-62

In many ways, we all have a travel story. Our lives, complete with twists and turns, ups and downs, detours, roadblocks, and forks in the road, tell our story.

Take a moment to think back over your life's journey. What have been the signifying markers along the way? Perhaps you remember a particularly challenging time, the day a new opportunity was presented, or the way you overcame a seemingly impossible obstacle. We all recall momentous events, such as the birth of a child, the death of a loved one, or meeting our spouse for the first time. Other seemingly minor events can be significant, too—a word spoken at the right time, a book we happened to pick up, a sermon we heard while driving.

These are all signifying markers in your life. They represent transitional moments and, in many cases, a life-altering choice. The choice you made set the trajectory for your future.

Jesus, too, made a choice.

Today's Gospel reading tells us that *"When the days drew near for [Jesus] to be taken up, he set his face to go to Jerusalem"* (9:51). Notice the resolve of Jesus. A face that is "set" is one steeled with intent and determination. Jesus' focus, gaze, and direction were resolute. Nothing would stop him from reaching his goal. Notice that, in setting his face to Jerusalem, Jesus was renouncing (setting his face *against*) all other directions. The "way" he chose was leading him in one direction only—to Jerusalem and to the Cross.

Not everyone in today's passage welcomes Jesus' intention. As Jesus passes through a village of Samaria, he sends his disciples ahead to announce his purpose. Yet they are rebuffed: *"But the people did not receive him, because his face was set toward Jerusalem"* (9:53).

The path of Jesus is difficult. Not everyone interested in Jesus is willing to travel his path. Some do not want to serve the Christ of God on his terms. They are more interested in their own mission. For a "sold out" disciple of Jesus, encountering people who reject the Lord can be painful. James and John suggest a "fire and brimstone" retribution for the Samaritan village that rejected Jesus. But Jesus makes it clear that loyalty to the kingdom of God will not be forced. Each person has a choice to make. Jesus simply moves on from those who do not welcome him.

The lack of openness toward Jesus in today's passage serves as a warning to us: If so many did not welcome Our Lord and still do not, should we expect any different? Probably not. Following Jesus on The Disciple's Way includes rejection. It is not a path of luxury and comfort either. In today's story we read, *"As they were going along the road, someone said to him, 'I will follow you wherever you go.' And Jesus said to him, 'Foxes have holes, and birds of the air have nests, but the Son of Man has nowhere to lay his head'"* (9:57-58).

Are you still willing to follow?

Perhaps an even tougher question than if you're willing to face rejection and forgo the creature comforts of house and home for Jesus, is whether you're willing to be as resolute as Jesus was in your intention. Are you willing to "set your face" as he did? To not waver? In today's reading, two potential disciples replied to Jesus' invitation with hesitation and qualification: *"…let me first go bury my father"* (9:59) and *"…let me first say farewell to those at my home"* (9:61).

The sovereign summons to follow Jesus along The Disciple's Way supersedes all other commitments, all other agendas, and all other plans. If you choose to follow Jesus, your course becomes his course. He is not looking for halfhearted disciples with divided loyalties. If you are in, you are *all in*, and in right now.

The movement from living in the kingdom of this world to living in the kingdom of God requires a whole-cloth change of our identity, relationships, behaviors, and life direction, a whole new "way" of living as a human being. Once you put your hand to the plow of God's kingdom, your face must remain set. You must keep your gaze straight ahead—no looking back.

REFLECT

Consider your own commitment to following Jesus. Can you think of a time in your life when you resolutely "set your face" to serve God, no matter what? Will you resolve to follow him today without hesitation, without looking back? If not, what is the "let me first _____" that is holding you back?

The Rev. Charlie Holt

RESPOND

_____

_____

_____

_____

Day 2

KINGDOM WORKERS / READ LUKE 10:1-20

There is an old saying: "You have to fish or cut bait." The original meaning is that you have to be doing something to help—either cast your line in the water or cut up bait for someone else.

On a fishing boat, everyone has a role to play. Some will be preparing lure, baiting hooks, or cleaning fish inside the boat, while others are focused outside the boat, working the lines and pulling in the catch. But no one gets to sit and do nothing! My wife enjoys fishing and catching, but not baiting and cleaning. I don't mind baiting her hook and cleaning the fish she catches. It's great to see her having fun and engaged in the activity of fishing.

Jesus calls his followers to an activity he likens to fishing—the activity of "catching people,"—of mission. Everyone has a role to play. In today's passage, Jesus stayed back and "cut the bait" while he sent seventy-two of his disciples on a great fishing expedition. Or, to use the metaphor in our text, Jesus sent out harvesters into a great field with an abundant crop of souls, ripe for harvesting.

Yet even as he sent them, Jesus said there was a problem. The harvest was plentiful, but the workers were few. More harvesters were needed. He asks his disciples to pray to the Lord to send out more.

I have often heard the complaint by hard-working lay ministers that only 20% of the people in the church do 100% of the work. Both cutting bait and reeling in fish is hard work. So is harvesting. When some are not doing their part, it is even harder, and frustrating. The power to mobilize the masses for mission starts, however, with prayer to the Lord and not complaint to the priest. The energy for mission in the Church is the Holy Spirit of God. It is the Lord's harvest field.

Notice that Jesus sent out the seventy-two knowing that more help was needed. He encouraged them to pray. What happened? The Lord of the harvest delivered. As these men entered various towns, they came upon houses of hospitality, populated with "sons of peace" (bait cutters). From these peaceful bases of hospitality and provision, the seventy-two were able to further their gospel work of missionary proclamation (fishers).

Again, not everyone is willing to help with the work of the kingdom. We should follow Jesus' example and work with those who are willing while "dusting off" those who aren't. Jesus will deal with them later. They aren't rejecting you; they are rejecting him—just as the one who welcomes you is welcoming the Lord. It really is all about Jesus:

> *"The one who hears you hears me, and the one who rejects you rejects me, and the one who rejects me rejects him who sent me."* Luke 10:16

But know this, kingdom work is exhilarating! Just like there is nothing more exciting than to reel in a fish, so there is nothing more thrilling than to witness a great harvest being reaped by the Lord's power.

When the missionaries returned to Jesus in today's passage, they were filled with excitement. You can hear it in their voices. *"The seventy-two returned with joy, saying, 'Lord, even the demons are subject to us in your name!'"* (10:17). Jesus said to them, *"I saw Satan fall like lightning from heaven"* (10:18). When God's people engage in mission, the spiritual forces of evil quake in their boots. Not even Satan, the highest form of evil, can remain in power when Jesus' people follow his call.

Friend, we have incredible power at our disposal to do good in this world for God. As Paul would teach later in his letter to the Ephesians, the Lord *"is able to do far more abundantly than all that we ask or think, according to the power at work within us"* (Ephesians 3:20). Let's pray to the Lord of the harvest to send more workers into the fields of abundance and expect great things!

REFLECT

How about you? Are you more of a bait-cutter or a fisherman? Do you enjoy working inside the church as a child of peace and hospitality? Or are you more like the seventy-two, an evangelist working in the fields? It's okay to be both. Ask the Lord to give you his power for your mission, wherever it is.

The Rev. Charlie Holt

RESPOND

_____

_____

_____

_____

Day 3

BLESSED EYES / READ LUKE 10:21-24

It's almost as if Jesus were giddy. His excitement over the success of the seventy-two disciples' mission overflows in today's passage with divine exuberance.

Nothing delights the heart of the Lord like seeing his people enthusiastically engaged in mission, liberating souls from Satan's bonds. As the disciples stepped out in faith, in the power of Jesus' call, their impact was stunning—there were cosmic repercussions—even the demons were subject to them. The joy of Jesus overflowed into praises to the Father at their happy return.

Oh, we were made for so much more! Many believers have limited their vocational focus too narrowly. Jesus would enlarge our vision and broaden our horizons so we can see the cosmic realities of his call to mission. We should ask the Lord for "blessed eyes" to see the revelation of the gracious will of God in our lives and in the world around us.

So often our lives are not fulfilling because we are not doing the things we were called, or even made, to do. But when a disciple of Jesus lives into his or her purpose and steps out toward the great adventure of the kingdom of God, it brings great blessedness and deep fulfilment. Our engagement in the adventure overjoys Jesus and the other two members of the Godhead.

In *Mere Christianity*, C.S. Lewis contemplates the community of the Triune God—Father, Son, and Holy Spirit—as a dramatic dance into which we gain access by faith.

> God is not a static thing—not even a person—but a dynamic, pulsating activity, a life, almost a kind of drama. Almost, if you will not think me irreverent, a kind of dance. The union between the Father and the Son is such a live concrete thing that this union itself is also a Person... What grows out of the joint life of the Father and Son is a real Person, is in fact the Third of the three Persons who are God.[1]

As God's creation, we are essentially the overflow of this unity and love of the Trinity. Their relationship is a dance of delight in one another. It's into this holy dance of joy that we have been called. C.S. Lewis again:

> The whole dance, or drama, or pattern of this three-Personal life is to be played out in each one of us: or (putting it the other way round) each one of us has got to enter that pattern, take his place in that dance. There is no other way to the happiness for which we were made.[2]

He continues:

> Good things as well as bad, you know, are caught by a kind of infection. If you want to get warm you must stand near the fire: if you want to be wet you must get into the water. If you want joy, power, peace, eternal life, you must get close to, or even into, the thing that has them... They are a great fountain of energy and beauty spurting up at the very centre of reality. If you are close to it, the spray will wet you: if you are not, you will remain dry. Once a man is united to God, how could he not live forever?[3]

---

1. C.S. Lewis, *Mere Christianity* (New York: Scribner, 1952), 136.
2. Lewis, *Mere Christianity*, 137.
3. Ibid.

Indeed, we were made to enter the dance of the Trinity. Nothing delights the heart of God more than to see us, his children, fulfilling the purposes for which he made us and joining in the dance of his divine will.

Here's the key for us to consider: choosing to follow on The Disciple's Way is to be willing to see the broad mission field with its abundant harvest and to step into it eagerly, ready to go to work with Jesus. Each day can be an adventure in mission as we make ourselves available to be used by God to do whatever he wants us to do—to take up the dance of his divine will.

I have a friend who sees every day as a kind of treasure hunt. She described to me how she wakes up with expectation, asking, "Okay, Jesus, what are we going to do today?" The wonderful thing is, God has the same attitude towards us. Jesus can't wait to rejoice with us when we return from our day's work excited over the treasures we've uncovered in doing his work of mission.

REFLECT

Are you ready to put on the "blessed eyes," to see as Jesus sees? To enter the dance and seek the treasures found in the Father's gracious will? Try expectantly praying, "Jesus, what are we going to do today?" Be open to the mission he gives you.

The Rev. Charlie Holt

RESPOND

_____

_____

_____

_____

Day 4

SEE AND DO / READ LUKE 10:25-37

It's one thing to see; it's another to do.

The problem with the lawyer in today's story is that he is willing to "do" for God and for others, but only within the narrow scope of who he "sees" as his neighbor—within his legalistic definition.

The lawyer asks Jesus *"…what shall I do to inherit eternal life?"* (10:25) Jesus invites him to answer his own question from the Law. The man responds with a summary of the two great commandments: Love God and love your neighbor. Jesus encourages him, *"[Do] this, and you will live"* (10:28).

But lawyers are all about details. The man wants to know: how expansive is the word "neighbor?" Like many of us, the lawyer would prefer to keep the law achievable within the bounds of his flesh, justifying himself. So he asks Jesus, *"And who is my neighbor?"* (10:29).

For a Jewish lawyer in Jesus' day, there were whole subsets of humanity that he'd rather not see as neighbors: Roman soldiers, Gentile interlopers, tax collectors, Samaritans, etc. The Samaritans provoked a particular prejudice due to a long history of bad blood between Judea in the south and Israel in the north, where the Samaritans lived (see the biblical books of Kings and Chronicles.) From a Jewish standpoint, Samaritans were corrupt family members. They were of mixed Gentile and Jewish blood and had polluted Judaism with idol worship (2 Kings 17:26-28).

Human beings struggle with prejudice. The question the lawyer poses, "And who is my neighbor?" betrays an attitude of his heart. Do I have to love everyone? Or do I get to exclude certain groups of people I don't like or who don't fit my into my comfort zone?

Jesus turned the question on its head.

He answers the question by telling the story of a rather nondescript man making a familiar journey from Jerusalem to Jericho. The man is mugged, robbed, and left for dead on the side of the road—all too familiar a scene at the time. The people you would expect to help, the Jewish leadership, see him and pass by without aid. Unexpected help comes from a Samaritan man who sees the victim, is moved by compassion, and goes above and beyond to minister to him at his own personal and sacrificial expense.

Here is the Jesus "twist." Hearers might conclude that Jesus was simply encouraging them to see the beaten man as their neighbor in need: don't neglect the guy on the side of the road. But that's not quite the moral of the story. Jesus asks, *"Which of these...proved to be a neighbor to the man?"* (10:36). Note the words: *"to the man?"* This turns the definition of "neighbor" around. It's one thing to ask, who would I be willing to minister *to*? It's quite another to ask, who would I be willing to receive ministry *from*? In effect, Jesus is asking, if you were left for dead on the side of the road, would it matter to you who was offering help?

I am reminded of President Ronald Reagan's famous exchange with the emergency room personnel after being shot in an attempted assassination. Being wheeled into the ER, Reagan joked, "I hope you are all Republicans." The doctors and nurses laughed, including the trauma team's lead physician, Dr. Joseph Giordano, a liberal Democrat, who quickly retorted, "Today, Mr. President, we are all Republicans."[4]

---

4. Del Quentin Wilber, *Rawhide Down: The Near Assassination of Ronald Reagan* (New York: Henry Holt and Company, 2011), 162.

When you are actively dying in an emergency room, the politics of the doctor don't really matter, do they? This is Jesus' point: *If we would receive help from anyone, shouldn't we be willing to give help to anyone?*

It is easy for us to pass by needs when we see them, and we see them every day. Somehow we do not relate; we do not *see* ourselves in the needs of others. Yet, here is the very heart of Jesus: he sees us, and he acts. "See" and "do." Jesus sees us beaten and laying on the side of the road, dead in our sins, and he identifies with us; he acts, by becoming the man left for dead:

> *"For our sake he made him to be sin who knew no sin, so that in him we might become the righteousness of God."* 2 Corinthians 5:21

Would you be willing to accept help from a liberal Democrat or a conservative Republican doctor? Personally, I'd welcome help from anybody with the willingness and skills to assist! But now, flip the question. Have you have consciously or unconsciously excluded any person or group from your love because they don't fit your definition of "neighbor?" Perhaps a personal enemy, a business rival, or a group with different beliefs from your own? It could be simple prejudice. Jesus calls you and me to turn this world upside down by turning the tables on our own prejudices (and we all have them).

Who was the neighbor to the man? The Samaritan—the one who was once considered an enemy. Beloved, you are the man. Though you were once at enmity with God, Jesus came to your aid. He saw your need, identified with you, and gave his life to make you whole. Now, go and do likewise.

REFLECT

Who around you have been left for dead on the side of the road? From a spiritual perspective, this is everyone. The collect for mission says Jesus "stretched out his arms of love on the hard wood of the cross that everyone might come within the reach of his saving embrace." Is there anyone you would exclude from his saving embrace? Who can you welcome in today?

The Rev. Charlie Holt

RESPOND

_____

_____

_____

_____

Day 5

HOW TO WELCOME JESUS / READ LUKE 10:38-42

I don't know about you but having people to my home is an opportunity for frantic cleaning.

I used to drive my children crazy running around and ordering them to "pick up that mess!" What would my guests think if my home was not neat and clean? While entering a home that is not in disarray is welcoming and peaceful, at times my focus was less on my guests than on my own pride.

In today's well-known passage, Jesus and his companions are continuing their journey to Jerusalem. They stop off in Bethany at the home of two sisters. This story of Martha and Mary is often used to make a distinction between action and contemplation. Much like the fellow monks of Thomas Merton who were chafed when he told them they were not really contemplatives but merely introverts, we can confuse a natural tendency to prefer listening over doing with a superior spirituality.

Yet, as we look closely at this sister story, there is more here than a commentary on our natural tendency toward either action or reflection. The story can help us evaluate our hearts and motivations as we seek to welcome Jesus and those who come in his name.

The story opens by telling us that Martha welcomed Jesus into her home. In this short phrase, we discover that the story is about hospitality. We also learn that Martha is an independent woman of means who can host this traveler. But very quickly we are given clues that the true host of the scene is Jesus. He is referred to by both Martha and the narrator as "Lord."

Mary's posture, sitting at his feet, reveals her deference to him. These clues reveal the authority Jesus carries in this home.

So, what does Jesus teach in this home of two sisters?

He continues to shake up the common understanding of how things should be. In yesterday's story of the Good Samaritan, Jesus pointed out that it was the despised Samaritan and not the religious leaders who did the will of God. In the story about Martha and Mary, Jesus again flips the expected and surprises us with a new way of seeing.

In the culture of the day, it was expected that women would serve men. That's just the way it was done. Even a woman of means like Martha would be expected to serve her visitor. To have a woman sit at the feet of a teacher as a disciple was unusual and possibly offensive to some. But Jesus' words in the passage clearly authenticate Mary's position as a disciple, learning from him.

Jesus' reprimand to Martha goes like this: *"Martha, Martha, you are anxious and troubled about many things, but one thing is necessary. Mary has chosen the good portion, which will not be taken away from her."*

Is Jesus here denigrating acts of service and love-in-action? No, he couldn't be. In the previous story of the Good Samaritan, he praises just this kind of action. What Jesus is doing here is showing that, in God's realm, women and men alike are welcomed and encouraged to become his disciples. And a critical part of discipleship is undistracted listening and devotion.

The way that Mary expresses her welcome of Jesus is to listen to his teaching. Unlike her distracted sister, Mary seems to hang onto his every word. She sees Jesus as the one who matters and seems to understand that to be his disciple means she must get to know his heart and mind.

Through listening to him, she will be changed into the person he is calling her to become.

When we welcome people into our lives, we allow them to affect us. When we are hospitable to the "others" in our midst, we take in what they offer. There is a vulnerability and openness when we listen to God and those he sends our way. Mary showed a willingness to be open to Jesus—an undistracted devotion.

Martha, on the other hand, was distracted by many things. Her focus was not so much on Jesus as on her own needs and tasks. Notice how many times in her complaint she uses the words *my* and *me*: *"Lord, do you not care that my sister has left me to serve alone? Tell her then to help me."*

Martha was self-focused, and she seemed to consider Jesus' authority as something she could manipulate to get her own way. Her service was not the problem; her focus was. I've been to many dinner parties where I've barely seen the hostess much less had a conversation with her. She is back in the kitchen making sure everything is perfect. As delicious and beautiful as these meals often are, I feel a loss at not having made a personal connection with this woman. While I can't judge the motive behind this type of hospitality, in Martha's case, Jesus is clear that where our hearts are focused is what matters.

To be a disciple of Jesus means we welcome him as the one who has real authority in our lives. We listen to him and those he sends our way; we allow them to change us. The contrast in this sister story makes clear that Jesus invites us to a better way of focusing on him and those who come from him as opposed to prioritizing our own agendas. This is how we walk with him along The Disciple's Way.

REFLECT

When it comes to your faith, are you more of a "be-er" or a "do-er?" Consider if your "being" or "doing" is more self-focused or Christ-focused. When in the past have you been vulnerable to those you've welcomed into your life? In what ways could you open yourself more to those God brings your way so that God can change you?

The Rev. Louise Samuelson

RESPOND

_____

_____

_____

_____

Day 6

DISCIPLES LEARN TO PRAY / READ LUKE 11:1-4

The Lord's Prayer is probably the most popular prayer of Christians.

Most of us were taught it as little children and can recite it from memory. It is appropriate both in times of celebration and mourning. It's even said by recovering alcoholics to close their 12-step meetings. I've seen people at death's door quietly mouth the words of this prayer as family and friends prayed over them. Often, we say it with rote recitation, barely cognizant of the words themselves.

This is the danger of memorized prayer. When we memorize, we hope that the words we learn will go deep into our consciousness. But there is also the possibility that they will come out of our mouths with little thought or reflection.

Jesus' disciples noticed his prayer life. They also knew it was the role of a master to teach his disciples. So they asked him to teach them to pray. The version of the "Our Father" most of us learned comes from the Gospel of Matthew. Today's version is found in Luke and can be a gift to those who want a fresh experience of the prayer that Jesus taught.

The first thing we notice in Jesus' prayer in Luke is that he teaches his disciples to address God as "Father." Throughout the Gospel of Luke, Jesus has been referring to God as *his* Father. Now he is inviting the disciples to see God in the same intimate way—as *their* Father. Through the use of this one word, Jesus lays the foundation of who his disciples are as his followers, including us. We are the *children* of God! He is our loving Father.

Jesus invites us into the familial relationship he has with God. Because God is now our Father, we can trust his love and care for us.

Next, Jesus teaches his disciples to start their prayer not with human needs but with a focus on God. Mary taught us in the previous story that the way to welcome and connect with Jesus is to focus on him foremost. Jesus instructs his disciples to first declare God's name as holy. The name of God represents who he is—God's being. God is holy and God's name is to be praised.

Luke's version of the prayer pairs God's being with God's action in the world: *"Father, hallowed be your name. Your kingdom come"* (11:2b). God's action is to bring his kingdom into being. Who God is and what God does are always connected.

Who we are and what we to do in relation to God are also connected. These are the subjects of the next couple of requests in Jesus' prayer. *"Give us each day our daily bread"* (11:3). This request expresses our reliance on God for our existence. We cannot live without God. We need food to eat as well as *"every word that proceeds"* from God's mouth as spiritual food (Matthew 4:4, NASB). God is the one who gives us life and enables us to be his children. Since we are his children, he feeds us and gives us our call to action.

God's kingdom coming into our lives brings us grace and forgiveness. As Jesus' disciples, we are forgiven and we are called to forgive the sins of others:

"...and forgive us our sins, for we ourselves forgive everyone who is indebted to us" (11:4a). As we grow in intimacy with God our Father through prayer, we become more like him. The love and forgiveness we experience from him creates in us the desire and power to pass that love and forgiveness on. The answer to our prayer for forgiveness becomes the answer to our prayer for God's kingdom to come, because it happens through us as we forgive.

The final request is: *"And lead us not into temptation"* or, as another version puts it, *"Keep us from falling into sin when we are tempted."* This request acknowledges our fallen human condition and the condition of the world, but also recognizes the surpassing power of God who can keep us from sin through his Spirit. He even promises to provide a way out when we are tempted (see 1 Corinthians 10:13).

I encourage you to spend some time meditating on Luke's version of the Lord's Prayer. Try using it instead of the more familiar version in your daily devotions this week and see how it might reignite the power and significance of Jesus' prayer. Notice especially the connection between *being* and *doing*, both in you and between you and God.

REFLECT

Meditate on and pray Luke's version of the Lord's Prayer. How do the subtle differences bring a freshness to what is so familiar? In what ways does focusing first on God's "being and doing" help you align your desires with his?

The Rev. Louise Samuelson

RESPOND

_____

_____

_____

_____

Day 7

RECEIVING GOOD GIFTS FROM THE FATHER /
READ LUKE 11:5-13

Have you ever fretted over a need you had, mustered up the courage to ask for help, and been surprised by how easy it was for someone to say yes?

When we really need something, we often think there is no one to whom we can turn. I remember times when my children came to me with financial requests, almost apologetically, for something they obviously needed but didn't have the means to buy. It hurt a little when they were so surprised that I would meet their need. Of course I want to help—I'm their mom!

In our last lesson, Jesus gave his disciples the words to pray when talking to God. By addressing God as Father, Jesus gave us the foundation for our relationship with God. Now Jesus goes on to unpack that relationship to help his disciples and us understand even more deeply what it means to be a child of God.

Jesus uses short stories to illustrate the point he is trying to get across about who God is in relation to us.

In the first story, we see someone asking a neighbor for bread on behalf of a visitor. We are back to our theme of hospitality. The setting is a community, a group of neighbors who are responsible to show hospitality to those who visit. There is resistance by the neighbor in the story to give the requested bread, but this resistance is finally overcome for the sake of peace in the community and in his own family. Even when there is resistance, we as humans often overcome it and know how to give. There is no resistance in God our Father! He desires to give freely to us.

The second story switches the orientation of the request. Now the disciples are placed in the position of the ones being asked. Jesus reminds them that they know how to respond with good things when asked by their children.

Even evil people will not give their children a snake instead of fish or a scorpion instead of an egg. There is no evil in God, so of course he wants to give good gifts to his children.

God knows we need physical food; but what Jesus is trying to teach his followers is that what God is waiting and desiring to give us *most* is God's self, the Holy Spirit. The Holy Spirit is our intimate connection to God. That's what our Father wants most—to be connected to us, to be with us and in us.

When we go to God in prayer, we need to wake up to the reality that there is no reluctance, resistance, or evil in God that keeps our Father from giving us what we need. God wants us to ask, seek, and knock in order that we can be ready and willing to receive all that he wants to give us. Asking, seeking, and knocking (which are other words for prayer) open up our hearts to God. When we go to God from a position of expectation and confidence, we can be ready for the flow of God's Spirit to move through us.

Prayer, in the way Jesus is teaching in this passage, becomes a conduit for God to be joined with us, his children. This is an incredibly powerful idea to consider: The God of the universe who created us in his image and then came to us as a human in Jesus Christ wants to be intimately connected to us through the Holy Spirit. This happens through prayer.

God our Father is always waiting, always ready, always willing to pour his Spirit into our lives. Our intimate connection with God through the Holy Spirit is the foundation of who we are as disciples of Jesus and is our power to walk along The Disciple's Way.

God is love and wants to give us all the goodness he is. Of course he does—he's our Father!

REFLECT

Spend some time imagining God your Father waiting with eagerness to give you good things. How does thinking about God as your loving Father eager to give you the Holy Spirit affect your attitude toward prayer? What are some ways you can keep on asking, seeking, and knocking to prepare your heart to receive all that God has for you?

The Rev. Louise Samuelson

RESPOND

Week Two

TRUE HEART

And I tell you, ask, and it will be given to you; seek, and you will find; knock, and it will be opened to you. For everyone who asks receives, and the one who seeks finds, and to the one who knocks it will be opened. What father among you, if his son asks for a fish, will instead of a fish give him a serpent; or if he asks for an egg, will give him a scorpion? If you then, who are evil, know how to give good gifts to your children, how much more will the heavenly Father give the Holy Spirit to those who ask him!

LUKE 11:9-13

CONSIDER

Do you have a true heart for the Lord and a deep desire for his Spirit to transform you?

Day 8

BEYOND MARVELING / READ LUKE 11:14-16

The journey to Jerusalem continues. After Jesus' powerful teaching on prayer, we are suddenly out in the open with Jesus doing what he does best—releasing the captives.

It can be jarring to go from focusing on God as our loving Father to this next scene in which Jesus is confronted with those who accuse him of being in league with the devil. In these three short verses, we encounter a mute man from whom Jesus casts a demon. Once he is set free, the man can speak again. Fantastic, right? Well, we are about to discover that on the road to Jerusalem, obstacles are in place.

Throughout the Gospel of Luke, God through Jesus moves toward those who are suffering. The Lord's deep compassion draws him to those who are imprisoned in ways that keep them from enjoying what God has for them.

The story of Jesus healing a mute man is the perfect illustration of what life is like for disciples who open their lives to the Father. We will be released from what is holding us, free to enjoy all God desires for us. But not all are open to God's freeing compassion. When his love is let loose in the world, people have different responses. As seen in the healing of the mute man, many will marvel. Others will try to explain it away. Yet others will ask for more signs.

We as humans have an almost insatiable desire to be amazed. Whether it is stories of incredible bodily feats or videos of close disasters, we get a rush out of being astonished. People were often amazed around Jesus.

However, marveling at the work or words of Jesus did not necessarily lead to faith. The people in the synagogue (where Jesus first initiated his ministry of release) were amazed one minute and ready to throw Jesus off a cliff the next. The religious leaders were amazed at Jesus' wisdom but kept trying to find a way to trap him.

Amazement does not equal faith. Nor does it equal action. When we are amazed, the action is "over there" and we are simply spectators. But the work of God in our midst calls for an active response. Simply standing and marveling isn't enough. Jesus invites us to *move*—to step out in faith, to follow him, and to participate with him in what he is doing rather than to simply watch from the sidelines.

It was obvious to the bystanders who heard the mute man speak that something powerful had happened. But some attributed this power to Satan. They were not able to believe that the power came from God, so they decided it must be evil. If, in fact, it was God who was using Jesus to set people free, that would demand a response from them. After all, they claimed to be children of God. Easier to explain it way. When our hearts are closed to receiving what God is bringing into the world, we will reframe the story so that we don't need to respond. This keeps us safe from obstacles along our road, but it also closes us off from what the Father wants to give to us.

Finally, some in the crowd wanted to test Jesus further. They demanded a sign from heaven—as if casting out a demon and hearing a mute man speak were not enough! For this group, nothing would ever be enough. It can be the same with us. We say: *Just one more answered prayer, Lord, and then I will believe. Just one more time getting me out of a tight spot; then I will follow you. I'm not quite sure you've done enough for me yet; when you do, I will be all yours.*

The evidence is already overwhelming. God is ready and willing to come and set you free through Jesus. Look around you. You have already seen enough to take a step of faith. When you are open to receiving all that God has for you, you will be set free and restored. When that happens, like the mute man, you will speak and God will be praised! You will want to help Jesus with his work of release in the world.

As Jesus' disciples, we must stay open to what he is doing. Notice when you are tempted to be amazed, but not engaged; to be critical, but not open; or to clamor for more evidence when you've already received all you could ever need. Trust the Holy Spirit and step out in faith. He will free you, and he will give you Jesus' moving compassion for all who need to be set free.

REFLECT

In what ways do you keep a distance from participating with God simply by being "amazed" at what he is doing? How are you reframing your own story so that God's work in your life does not seem evident? Try retelling your story with God at the center. When will you have enough of God to take the next step he's calling you to as his disciple?

The Rev. Louise Samuelson

RESPOND

_____

_____

_____

_____

Day 9

A WELL-SWEPT HOUSE / READ LUKE 11:17-26

In today's reading, Jesus unpacks the good work he did in setting the mute man free that we read about yesterday.

Jesus was accused of using evil to drive out the man's demon. Now he uses logical arguments to counter this attack. If he is casting out demons by the prince of demons, Satan, then the house of Satan is divided against itself and would fall. Further, he counters, *"...by whom do your sons cast [demons] out?"* (11:19). If the crowd believes their sons cast out evil through God's power, they must accept that Jesus does, too—they have to be consistent. In fact, Jesus is teaching them that doing good is, in fact, doing *good*. Wherever evil and oppression are vanquished, that is where the kingdom of God is.

Jesus sets up a clear dualistic perspective when it comes to good and evil. There is no neutrality. There are people who work alongside Jesus to set others free from what keeps them trapped and shackled (good), and there are those who do not, or even oppose this work (evil). Standing still in the face of the darkness you encounter is actually standing *with* evil. But everyone who offers a way to freedom through Christ is in God's service, standing for *good*. To be a follower of Jesus, to be with Jesus, means that you act on behalf of those who are ensnared in circumstances that harm and oppress them.

But how do we do that? So often we feel the heaviness of our own oppression and lack of freedom. How can we work to set others free when we don't feel free ourselves?

While Jesus sets up a duality regarding being good and evil, we experience both in our everyday lives. We know ourselves to be a mixture of light and dark, good and evil, love and hate. So the point is not to see ourselves as either all good or all evil (we are sinners still in the process of being made holy). It's for us to realize there is no *standing still* on The Disciple's Way. We are either moving toward God (and the good) or away from him. Even as we struggle against evil, we can make steady progress toward God.

Jesus uses the image of a house swept clean to help us more fully understand this concept.

Jesus is the one who has the power to enter our lives and make real change. He comes in and sweeps us clean. Through his suffering and victory at Calvary, he has already released us from the control of evil. He has forgiven our sins, once for all time. He continues to bind up our wounds, heal our brokenness, and give us what we need. Jesus wants to do a complete work in us. He wants every room, every hidden closet, every dusty corner of our lives to be swept clean. He is greater than our fears, our addictions, even our doubts and disinterest. But are we ready for such a deep cleansing? Or are we more interested in just a bit of surface dusting?

In today's text, Jesus is the strongest one who comes and sets us free (11:22). But if we don't continue to furnish our home with the things that invite Jesus into greater and greater ownership, we are in danger of letting other forces move in.

What are ways we can fill our lives with things of God's kingdom? How can we partner with Christ and allow him to clear out the clutter we love to hoard?

In previous lessons, we looked at how a focus on Jesus and his word through prayer and study are essential for discipleship. In addition, being involved in setting captives free is also a way to be with Jesus. Participating with him in his kingdom work will keep us moving toward God. Our house will continue to become a place that is not only swept clean but is roomy and spacious enough for others to find respite.

REFLECT

The touch of God brings power for an entirely new way of life. How has Jesus delivered you from evil, freed you from bondage, and swept your house clean? What areas of your life are you keeping hidden from the finger of God, desiring to be a little better but not completely transformed? Invite Jesus now to clean out everything that will hinder you along The Disciple's Way.

The Rev. Louise Samuelson

RESPOND

Day 10

FOLLOWERS, NOT FANS / READ LUKE 11:27-28

Today we read the final two verses of the story in which Jesus casts a demon from a man who was unable to speak.

For three days we have explored what happens when God's power breaks through into the world. We noted that there are several unhelpful responses. Some people simply marvel at God's power from the sidelines. Others deny it is God altogether. Still others ask for even more evidence that God is at work. Each of these responses keep people from fully entering into God's realm.

In today's verses, a woman in the crowd praises the womb that bore Jesus and the breasts that nursed him. While this woman seems to be giving Jesus praise and adoration, he has no interest in her words. Just as the man Jesus set free from an evil spirit earlier in Luke is more than a prop for an argument, Jesus knows his mother is more than breasts and a womb. Jesus always looks to the person and not what they can do for him.

Jesus was raised by the woman who is our supreme example (except for Jesus himself) of how a human being submits wholeheartedly to God. In Luke 1:38 we read, *"And Mary said, 'Behold, I am the servant of the Lord; let it be to me according to your word.'"* Mary is the one who allowed God to be born through her so he could enter the world and be with us. She was the one who would eventually allow her soul to be pierced at the foot of the Cross, watching her beloved son suffer for us all. Mary is not simply an example of a biological necessity; she is what a follower of God should look like. So when Jesus retorts that *"'Blessed rather are those who hear the word of God and keep it!'"* (11:28) he knows his mother exemplifies exactly what he is talking about.

I often wonder how Jesus feels watching us come to praise him with songs and prayers on Sunday morning. We sing over and over again lines about how great Jesus is. We lift his name on high and love to sing his praises, but do we love to hear the word and keep it?

Sometimes praising Jesus can be a way for us to keep him at a distance. When we lift him on high, are we actually putting him beyond our everyday lives? When we set him apart with our Holy, Holy, Holy's, do we remove him from the reality of where we really live? Is our love for praise more about making ourselves feel good than about what Jesus desires from us? When we drive away from church, are we allowing the word we heard to speak to our hearts? What do we do with those moments in which we feel conviction or calling?

Jesus is not looking for fans. He is looking for followers—those who will join him in his mission work. God did not come near to us and dwell among us so we could push him away and live however we want. Being an insider in the church crowd, saying the right words, moving with the pack—these are not the marks of a disciple.

Jesus is not looking for people who can put on a good show, who can act out what might look like faith. He is looking for people who are truly full of faith—those willing to join him in releasing the ones held captive and restoring the ones who are fractured. Jesus wants us to continue the expansion of God's loving mission in the world, right where we live, right here, and right now.

REFLECT

In your worship, are you elevating Jesus to where he is removed from your everyday reality? How can your praise of Jesus instead help you become more sensitive to his call on your life? What would help you move from being an observer to a participant in Jesus' work? Ask him for it. Consider examples in your life of those who hear the word of God and keep it.

The Rev. Louise Samuelson

RESPOND

_____

_____

_____

_____

Day 11

LIVING IN THE LIGHT / READ LUKE 11:29-36

People often say they want a sign from God in order to know what to do.

When my job in Brownville, Texas, was coming to an end, I asked God for a sign. I sent out twenty-four letters to Episcopal churches looking for a priest. I asked God to open the right door and keep the rest closed. I received only one response. It was from St. John the Divine in Houston. They offered me a job.

God had answered my prayer; he had given me a sign—only one response. About four months later, I complained to my wife that I should have gotten more job offers. So much for my appreciation of the sign! How often are the signs we ask God for not really about wanting to know God's will.

Evidently there was widespread demand for Jesus to give a sign to the crowds to prove his identity. If you had heard of a man named Jesus walking on water, miraculously feeding thousands of people, and making the mute speak, wouldn't you want to witness one of his miracles? I would. God, however, was not going to give a sign apart from Jesus himself. The only sign this crowd would be given was the sign of Jonah.

In the pagan city of Nineveh, about 750 years before the birth of Jesus, the prophet Jonah's preaching led the entire city to repentance. The king of Nineveh declared that every person was to fast from food and water, dress in sackcloth, and turn away from their evil ways. Even the animals were dressed in sackcloth and fasted. Jonah's mission was a huge success!

Now, Jesus too was calling people to repentance. But rather than perform the kind of sign requested by the people to prove his identity, Jesus chose his own sign—what he calls the "sign of Jonah."

What is this "sign of Jonah?" It is Jesus' coming Resurrection. Just as Jonah came out of the fish alive after three days, so Jesus would emerge from the grave after three days; only, better than Jonah, he would have been raised from the dead! Jesus' Resurrection will be a powerful sign to the people. But neither Jesus' preaching nor this "sign of Jonah" will bring about repentance in *all* the people of Jesus' day, especially those within the leadership of Israel.

Jesus realizes that the people of his day, the people of Israel to whom he has been sent, do not comprehend who he is. They are in darkness. He states that the Queen of Sheba and the people of Nineveh, who were all Gentiles, understood God and their own sin nature better than these Jews do.

In the section that follows, Jesus shifts gears and speaks metaphorically about the eye being the lamp of the body. Our eyes work by allowing light to flow into them; when light flows in, we can see. But when our eyes are impaired, we are literally in darkness and cannot see. Lack of sight impairs other bodily functions as well.

Morally, the eyes of our hearts are to be fixed on good and not evil. Good is the light that will penetrate our being and enable us to function as God desires. We take care not to corrupt ourselves by gazing at evil, literally or figuratively.

There is a connection between this metaphor of light Jesus employs and the request of the people for a "sign." The crowd is not focusing on Jesus as the Light of the World and on his salvific work among them. Instead, they are focused on testing Jesus—and so, doubting him.

The great work of Satan in the Garden of Eden was to get Adam and Eve to doubt God's command. The people of Israel were now doubting Jesus. They doubted that he was their Messiah, their rescuer, sent by God to find the lost sheep and to call all people to repentance. No wonder they accuse Jesus of being in league with Satan. Their eyes are impaired by their doubt and so their understanding is full of darkness.

REFLECT

Are there any sins you want God to "root out" of you that keep you from living fully in the light of Jesus? Ask God to remove them and sow understanding in your heart instead. Then you can act in truth and love, serving others and keeping the commandments of Christ, the Light of the World.

The Rev. Reagan Cocke

RESPOND

Day 12

THE ATTEMPT TO REDEFINE GOD / READ LUKE 11:37-54

Have you ever acted morally superior to someone over something that was ultimately meaningless?

At the time of Jesus, there was a man-made rule followed by the Pharisees to preserve ceremonial purity. Before eating, water was poured over the hands to remove the defilement of coming into contact with a sinful world. Jesus did not partake of this ceremony prior to his dinner with the Pharisee; his host was astonished. Jesus said, *"Now you Pharisees cleanse the outside of the cup and of the dish, but inside you are full of greed and wickedness"* (11:39).

The Pharisees were concerned with what one does *outwardly*—with external forces and events. Jesus is concerned with who one is *inwardly*—with internal thoughts and motives. Jesus wants a right inner attitude. In this dinner dialogue, he is trying to teach the Pharisee that no amount of water can make up for a corrupted inner life. When we concentrate on the external, we overlook the critical internal—our heart attitude to God, which should direct all our actions.

The Pharisees loved being in the public eye, sitting in prominent and distinctive seats, being addressed respectfully in public, and being shown deference. They complied lists of rules outside God's law that required the people to do very difficult things. But then they did not help the people to follow these rules. They seemed to put up random "moral" barriers around God. They lacked love while majoring in judging others.

One such rule erected by the Pharisees was that a person could not come into contact with a grave without incurring defilement. Even walking over an unmarked grave made one unclean. But how was one to know if the grave was unmarked?

This is just one example of how the Pharisees turned God's Law into a list of obscurities and riddles only they, the experts, could explain. Rather than opening up the treasure of God's Word, they prevented ordinary people from coming near to God, whom they truly desired to know. This holier-than-thou attitude caused Jesus to condemn them with a series of woes.

The first two woes accuse the Pharisees of being preoccupied with the minutiae of the law and people's opinions of them rather than the wellbeing of those under their leadership. The third woe targets the lawyers who add burdens to the people but do nothing to help them carry these weights. The fourth woe accuses Israel's leaders of conspiring to kill the prophets. And the fifth woe reveals their misunderstanding of Jesus himself, to which they add the greater sin of keeping the people from the knowledge of Jesus.

Ironically, the Pharisees were supposed to be the experts in God's Law and examples to God's people. They had become the exact opposite. They saw their job now as lying in wait to trap Jesus. If only they could catch him in one little slip, one mistake, he could be imprisoned and, perhaps, executed.

The Pharisees' problem was that they were trying to redefine God. God was there in their midst, defining himself, and they missed him altogether. They were not the first. This, in fact, was the first human sin. Adam and Eve tried to redefine God and his commands when they ate from the tree of the knowledge of good and evil. They failed…miserably, and so will we if we try to remake God in our own image.

REFLECT

Do you have a similar problem to the Pharisees? Perhaps God is working in your life and you are missing him because you're trying to redefine who he is and how he is to act. Take some time to ask God to help you acknowledge him in the midst of your daily life and be obedient to his leading, rather than trying to redefine him according to your terms.

The Rev. Reagan Cocke

RESPOND

_____

_____

_____

_____

Day 13

OPEN HEARTS / READ LUKE 12:1-12

Have you ever been caught up in a crowd? Crowds can be entertaining and energizing, but they can also be disorienting and destructive. Crowds can take on a life of their own.

At the University of Pennsylvania, our football team won only one game my freshman year, which was their usual record before I matriculated. In my sophomore year, we flipped the stats. Instead of going 1-11, we went 11-1. I was there in historic Franklin Field when we beat Harvard to win the Ivy League Championship outright.

When the game was over, we students poured onto the field. In celebration, we tore down the goalpost in the east endzone, paraded it out onto South Street, and headed to the bridge over the Schuylkill River. Once there, the crowd threw the goalpost into the river. While that caused enough confusion and damage, some decided to take things further and began flipping cars parked on nearby streets in the name of celebratory victory. Yes, crowds can take on a life of their own. In this case, an initial joyful celebration became host to a secondary carnival of destructive evil.

While Jesus often draws large crowds to himself, he also realizes their limits and dangers. He takes time to get away from the crowds by himself and also with a smaller group of his disciples, who are of first importance to him when it comes to teaching. On one such occasion, in today's text, Jesus talks to his disciples about the leaven of the Pharisees.

Jesus speaks here about a part of the bread-making process that is slow, constant, and thorough. When leaven is added to dough, it slowly and gradually permeates the dough and transforms it. The leaven of the Pharisees, warns Jesus, is hypocrisy—saying one thing and doing another. This practice of appearing righteous on the outside while keeping a hard heart toward God is insidious. It is subtle and gradual; its harmful effects can spread if unchecked.

Verses 2 and 3 should give all followers of Jesus a profound gut check: *"Nothing is covered up that will not be revealed, or hidden that will not be known. Therefore whatever you have said in the dark shall be heard in the light, and what you have whispered in private rooms shall be proclaimed on the housetops."*

We cannot hide from God—something the "Collect for Purity" at the beginning of the Holy Communion service from the Book of Common Prayer states so well:

> *Almighty God, to you all hearts are open, all desires known, and from you no secrets are hid: Cleanse the thoughts of our hearts by the inspiration of your Holy Spirit, that we may perfectly love you, and worthily magnify your holy Name; through Christ our Lord.* AMEN.
>
> — Book of Common Prayer, p. 323

After warning his disciples to beware the leaven of the Pharisees, Jesus goes on to encourage his disciples not to fear these hypocrites. He says that those who can kill only your body have no more power over you after you are dead. Their power is limited; God's is not.

Jesus wants us to look at the bigger picture. There is a place for fear in our relationship to God, grounded in this fact: we are always ready to sin, in spite of and even in the face of our recognition of the greatness and righteousness of God. However, as we come into the perfect love of God, as revealed in the death and Resurrection of Jesus (which is yet to happen in this passage from Luke 12), his perfect love will cast out our fear. It will bring us into a place of loving obedience. (Note: We are told to fear God with a reverent awe. We are never told to fear Satan—only to be aware of his tactics and to resist him.)

Jesus continues his teaching by sharing the profound concern God has for each of us as individuals: *"...even the hairs of your head are all numbered"* (12:7).

He then goes on to leave no doubt that our attitude toward Jesus determines our eternal status. People who reject Jesus reject God. He warns his disciples that they will be brought before the synagogues and rulers for holding this belief. But they are not to fear because the Holy Spirit will give them the words to speak—the Spirit of God will be their ever-ready helper.

REFLECT

When has the Holy Spirit helped you in the spur of the moment to know what to say or do? Consider your history with God and how he has been walking beside you, even when you might not have felt it. God sees and knows everything. Ask God what areas of your heart you need to willingly open to his loving touch, in faith, right now.

The Rev. Reagan Cocke

RESPOND

Day 14

WORRY AND TRUST / READ LUKE 12:13-42

When someone dies, there are always people ready to enrich themselves.

There is the story of an old, wealthy man who left his inheritance to no one. Instead, he arranged for an auction to sell off his estate before doing the same with his house and property. The auction began with a small portrait of the man's son, who had died years before. Only one bid came from the gathered crowd; they were looking for deals on the more expensive and impressive items. The bidder was the man's faithful servant who had helped raise the son. With the purchase of the small portrait, the auction came to an abrupt halt. The old man had left the following instructions: "Whoever purchases the portrait of my son, that person will receive my entire estate as well."

The old servant had no thought of inheriting the entire estate! He was only interested in the memento to help him remember the young man he had loved. He valued relationship over wealth and, because of this, received both.

In this next section of Luke, we find a man valuing wealth over relationship. He asks Jesus to decide an inheritance case in his favor, but Jesus rejects his request and uses the opportunity to teach.

Beware of covetousness, Jesus warns, for *"one's life does not consist in the abundance of his possessions"* (12:15). Jesus came to bring people to God, not possessions to people. The thinking of the man was most likely that he wanted to be in control of his own future, even at the expense of God and others.

Jesus says that people who are not rich toward God are fools. Covetousness reveals the attitude of your heart.

From the sins of greed and selfishness, Jesus turns to the sin of worry. Apparently some of his disciples were anxious about things. You may ask why worrying is a sin. It's because worrying leads you away from trusting in God. Jesus reasons that if God makes provisions for the ravens (considered unclean birds), how much more for you who are created in *his image*? Or, if you cannot extend your lifespan even a minute, why do you think you can control other things? If God delights in adorning flowers that disappear quickly, won't he do much more for you?

Worry inhibits positive action; it can also lead to destructive action. Instead of worrying, Jesus' disciples are to pledge themselves to him and spend their time doing his work and seeking his rule in their lives and in the world. They are to bring others into the same relationship with and understanding of Jesus. They will not grow rich, but they will not go lacking either. Just as the man in the opening story discovered, when we have the son, we will be given everything else we need, including spiritual riches beyond measure.

As believers, we are not to be dominated by our possessions. Trust in riches prohibits trust in God. Neither are we to worry about our lack of possessions. This fear creates stress and paralysis. Instead we are to trust God for what we need while we seek true and eternal treasure. This is The Disciple's Way.

REFLECT

If you were to rank yourself on a "worry scale" from 0 to 10, where would you be? Whatever your result, take it to God in prayer. Lay your worries at the foot of the Cross. Ask God's Spirit to strengthen your trust in him as you release the worry (or trust in possessions) that keeps you at a distance from God.

The Rev. Reagan Cocke

RESPOND

_____
_____
_____
_____

Week Three

REALISTIC FAITH

There were some present at that very time who told him about the Galileans whose blood Pilate had mingled with their sacrifices. And he answered them, "Do you think that these Galileans were worse sinners than all the other Galileans, because they suffered in this way? No, I tell you; but unless you repent, you will all likewise perish. Or those eighteen on whom the tower in Siloam fell and killed them: do you think that they were worse offenders than all the others who lived in Jerusalem? No, I tell you; but unless you repent, you will all likewise perish.

LUKE 13:1-5

CONSIDER

Is your faith anchored in the unseen reality of God's kingdom or in the fleeting here-and-now?

Day 15

FAITHFULNESS WITHIN THE HOUSEHOLD OF GOD
/READ LUKE 12:35-48

Have you ever been given a simple task and blown it?

A few years ago I was in San Antonio for a doctor's appointment with my mother. She had suffered two concussions in six-months. After some tests, her doctor was ready to give her a suggested treatment plan and explain where she was in her recovery. My younger sister, a doctor, thought it wise for one of us to be there to talk with the doctor. After 30 minutes of waiting, I took a brief restroom break; when I returned, the doctor had come and gone. I had blown it! My only mission was to talk with the doctor, and I had missed him.

In this instance, there were thankfully no significant consequences as the physician's assistant came in and updated me on everything. I could now give my sister a full report.

But, according to Jesus' teaching in this next section of Luke's travel narrative, failing to be ready for his return does have consequences. We need to be aware of what will happen. The consequence of not being ready for Jesus' return is judgment. Not being ready means being outside the will of God. It is like going on vacation and forgetting all about your job or abandoning your family. Not being in the will of God means forgetting your calling as a disciple of Jesus and abandoning the family of God.

While this Parable of the Watching Servants in Luke is primarily a reference to being prepared for the second coming, it can also be understood as a warning from Jesus to his disciples of a coming crisis—namely, his crucifixion and/or the destruction of Jerusalem in A.D. 70. I think we need to keep all three events in mind as we read the passage. They reinforce one another because each one fulfills a prophecy in chronological order and shows that God is in control and consistent with his Word. The events are all judgment events: the crucifixion (judgment of sin), the destruction of Jerusalem (judgment of Israel), and the second coming (Jesus will judge all humanity). Followers of Jesus are to live in constant readiness, even in the midst of crisis.

Peter asks Jesus to whom he is addressing this parable. Jesus does not answer directly. Instead, he responds that the greater the privilege of his followers, the greater their responsibility.

The household manager in the parable proves himself trustworthy, obedient, and righteous. He will be given additional responsibilities. However, when a servant abuses the trust placed in him, upon the unexpected return of the master, he will be punished with a severe penalty and downgraded to join the unfaithful. People will be punished not only for doing wrong, but also for not doing what is right.

The great English Anglican bishop J.C. Ryle writes that, "Our very ignorance is part of our sin."[5] Australian New Testament scholar Leon Morris adds, "God's servant must make every effort to find out what God's will is and do it. All are accountable."[6] Readiness for a disciple means living within the will of God in our daily lives, ever listening for his leading and ever ready to respond to his call.

---

[5] John Charles Ryle, *Expository Thoughts on the Gospels, St. Luke, 2 vols.* (New York: Robert Carter & Brothers, 1875; London: James Clark and Co., 1969).

[6] Leon Morris, *Luke: An Introduction and Commentary* (Downers Grove, IL: InterVarsity Press, 1974; Grand Rapids, MI: Wm. B. Eerdmans Publishing Co., 2000), p. 239.

REFLECT

How do you know what God's will is for you? One easy and obvious answer is to read the Bible and follow the teachings of Jesus. When we do this, we realize how much help we need! This sense of need leads us to be in prayer with the Father. Below is a good prayer to use:

> *Hold us fast, O Lord of Hosts, that we fall not from thee. Grant us thankful and obedient hearts, that we may increase daily in the love, knowledge, and fear of thee. Increase our faith and help our unbelief; that being provided for and relieved of all our needs by thy fatherly care and providence, we may live a godly life, to the praise and good example of thy people, and after this life may reign with thee for ever; through Jesus Christ our Savior.[7]*

— James Pilkington, Bishop of Durham, 1520-1576

The Rev. Reagan W. Cocke

RESPOND

_____

_____

_____

_____

---

[7]. *The SPCK Book of Christian Prayer* (London: Society for Promoting Christian Knowledge, 1996), p. 206.

Day 16

THE COMING CRISIS / READ LUKE 12:49-59

Lack of planning can be disastrous.

After hurricane Katrina devastated New Orleans in August 2005, Hurricane Rita fired up in the Gulf of Mexico just a month later. The citizens of Houston were on edge.

Rita appeared to be on a path to wipe out Galveston before wreaking destruction on the Bayou City. My family and I determined to evacuate to San Antonio to stay with my parents. Unfortunately, most of Houston decided to leave around the same time we did. For many, the normally three-hour trip took up to twelve hours! By taking a less obvious route into the storm's track (before it arrived) and then turning south, we were able to make the journey in six hours. Still, it was obvious Houston was not built for a mass evacuation. In the months and years ahead, new evacuation routes were planned to get more people out of Houston in an organized way.

So, twelve years later, when Hurricane Harvey arrived, was Houston prepared? No! The storm devastated the city. All the planning discussions of the previous years seemed to be in vain. There was not an evacuation plan in place and the city had not prepared for the rainfall and subsequent flooding many had predicted over the years. The coming crisis was essentially ignored. Lives were lost, and millions of people paid the price of the destruction with 135,000 homes damaged or destroyed and a million cars ruined.

Jesus knows a crisis is coming. He has told his disciples to be ready for it. Now he turns his attention to the Cross, the first crisis he has been referring to. The Cross will be the place where God's judgment comes to bear on sin. Jesus is the representative of humanity. He likens his coming crucifixion to a baptism. People are baptized for the removal of their sins. God's plan for salvation is through judgement, brought upon the innocent body of Jesus, to destroy sin and death and thereby save the world.

The Cross of Jesus, however, will divide people—even within families. Though Jesus is called the Prince of Peace (Isaiah 9:6), the peace he brings is between God and humanity, not necessarily between people. Jesus warns his disciples that there may be divisions in their own families over him.

Jesus then accuses his fellow Jews of concentrating on superficial things and not on the purposes and movement of God. There is a major problem with sin in the world, yet these Jews do not see it. They can read the signs of the weather, but not of the coming destruction and advent of God's kingdom—even when it is right in front of them. Instead, Israel's religious leaders are arguing over whether it's lawful for Jesus to heal on the Sabbath. They are missing the true significance of Jesus' presence!

In the final section, Jesus reminds the crowd that it is wise to get the best settlement possible out-of-court instead of taking a hopeless case before a judge. In the same way, they ought to make peace with God while there is still time.

Jesus' teaching here is not about purgatory (getting the best settlement you can), as some have claimed, but about realizing that Jesus is your advocate, your pro bono counsel! Jesus does not want his listeners or us to miss out on his extraordinary offer to take up our cause at Calvary as our legal advocate *and substitute* to save us from the coming destruction.

Reflect

Have you ever gone to court? Were you prepared ahead of time? We would not think of going to court without preparation, so why would we neglect to make sure we're prepared for the return of Jesus? What are you doing now in preparation for his return? Have you accepted Jesus' advocacy and substitution on your behalf? Thank him for it now with a grateful heart.

The Rev. Reagan W. Cocke

RESPOND

_____

_____

_____

_____

Day 17

REPENTANCE AND GOD'S PATIENCE /
READ LUKE 13:1-9

> *Though waves and storms go o'er my head,*
> *Though strength and health and friends be gone,*
> *Though joys be withered all, and dead,*
> *Though every comfort be withdrawn,*
> *On this my steadfast soul relies, —*
> *Father! Thy mercy never dies.*[8]
>
> —Johann A. Rothe, 1799-1867

Life is tough.

We are hit daily with disappointments and challenges not of our own making. From the loss of a loved one to a difficult client, employee, or boss; from a destructive storm to a ruthless scammer; from the betrayal of a friend to the rebellion of a child—life has its challenges.

One of the things that frustrates me is when people try to come up with reasons why unfortunate things happen to people. This practice is not only insensitive, it assumes that people deserve what they get because they are not diligent enough, smart enough, or proactive enough. People who

---

8. *The SPCK Book of Christian Prayer*, 41.

invent such reasons may be unconsciously keeping themselves from the uncomfortable reality that harmful events happen in this life. It's part of living in a broken world. Jesus seems to agree that this kind of thinking is unhealthy as he reiterates our need to repent and return to God.

In today's passage, some people bring up a murderous event to try to engage Jesus. They want him to make a judgment about the sinfulness of the victims of Pontius Pilate (of whom Jesus will soon be a victim). Jesus uses the opportunity to drive home the point about the urgency of repentance.

Once again, Jesus is turning things on their head. The common thinking of the day was that bad things happened to bad people—these victims were surely deserving of their deaths at the hands of Pilate. In his response, Jesus takes universal sinfulness as a given. The fate of those killed is a warning to all to repent and be in a right relationship with God because, though hardship in this world is unpredictable, coming judgment is sure.

Repentance in Scripture is a key part of both our salvation and our sanctification.

Salvation means we have been saved. According to the New Testament, salvation is coming into a right relationship with Jesus. It is accepting his death upon the Cross as a propitiation for our sins. Propitiation means atonement. The word atonement means reparation for a wrong or injury. It is helpful to see the combination of English words: *at-one-ment*. Atonement can be thought of as being "at one" with God—being reconciled to him. God was satisfied in the event of the Cross, allowing reconciliation between himself and his people—our salvation.

Sanctification is the ongoing process of our being made new by the Holy Spirit who lives in us. In this process, we grow in Christ-likeness, meaning we are to look and become progressively more like Jesus in our thinking and behavior. As the Holy Spirit prompts and convicts us, we are to make choices in keeping with our identity in Christ. The Spirit gives us the power to do this.

Repentance is a step in our salvation (realizing our need to be saved from our sins and being willing to turn from them). Repentance is also part of the continuing rhythm of sanctification (turning from each new sin as we encounter it and going in the other direction).

To bring the point home about the need for repentance, Jesus tells the Parable of the Barren Fig Tree. It explores two themes: the need for repentance and God's slowness to punish. There is no indication the fig tree will ever bear fruit. It is taking up room where a productive tree can be planted. The vinedresser who cares for the fig tree counsels the owner to have patience and let him continue caring for the tree one more season. The vinedresser declares he will take no initiative in destroying the tree but says the owner may cut it down himself if it remains barren next season.

The fact that evil is not punished here and now does not mean that God approves of what sinners are doing. It means that God is merciful and patient, desiring for all to come to repentance. His mercy never dies.

REFLECT

How has God been merciful and patient with you in your life? Where is God calling you to be merciful and patient with others? After all, if we cannot be merciful and patient with others, can we really understand how merciful and patient God is with us?

The Rev. Reagan W. Cocke

RESPOND

_____

_____

_____

_____

Day 18

THE UNSETTLING PRESENCE OF THE KINGDOM /
READ LUKE 13:10-21

Have you ever shouted, "Hallelujah" in church?

There is a story of a woman who came to church for the first time and heard a sermon on the Cross, the way to heaven. She was so overcome that she shouted "Hallelujah!" in the middle of the service. An usher came rushing up and whispered in her ear not to talk during the sermon. "But," she said, "I've just found salvation!" The usher replied, "Well, you can't find that here."

In today's story, Jesus is worshiping in a synagogue. This is the final time the Gospels record Jesus in a synagogue—a setting where he'd engaged in continuing disputes with his opponents. Just like the usher, the synagogue ruler is none too pleased with Jesus' behavior.

A woman who could not stand, perhaps from a fused spine causing her much pain, enters for worship. There is no indication she knew or believed in Jesus. But when Jesus touches her and enables her to stand again, she recognizes the source of her healing and begins praising God. The woman's healing and vocal praise annoy the synagogue ruler; more than annoy—he is "indignant." Why? Because the healing took place on the Sabbath. He considered what Jesus did to be "work" and, therefore, forbidden on the Sabbath.

Nowhere in Scripture can one find a prohibition against healing people on the Sabbath. The Sabbath laws were given by God for people to have a day of rest that focused on their relationship with God. And here is God, among his people, seeing a woman in pain and healing her, without her even asking—something everyone should give praise for, not just this woman. Yet, there is backlash.

Interestingly, Jesus points out the fact that the rabbis had created loopholes in the law to take care of animals on the Sabbath. Jesus chastises them for caring more about animals than people. Additionally, the animals Jesus mentions seem to be personal animals used for work and transport. So, his critics are putting their own needs above the good of others. The rabbi's first call is always to care for those he serves; and this woman is a Jew! Thus, Jesus points out, the rabbis have failed in their calling and are not reflecting the love of God.

Jesus states that this woman's condition is a result of Satan's "bonds." He does not call her evil but portrays her as a victim of the enemy. Jesus had come to overthrow Satan and was doing so even as they watched.

Jesus was also trying to get the Jewish leaders to grasp exactly what the Sabbath means. God rested on the Sabbath because all his creation work was finished and was good. Yet, the influence of Satan and sin has corrupted God's good creation. There is work to be done, and Jesus is doing that work to restore God's creation. But these people were blind to it. The woman sees it and praises God, which is what we are all called to do on the Sabbath. The religious leader opposes it.

Public opinion, however, was on Jesus' side; the kingdom was having an impact! While his adversaries were put to shame, the people *"rejoiced at all the glorious things that were done by him"* (13:17).

The point of the short Parable of the Mustard Seed, which immediately follows this healing, is to illustrate the wondrous expansion of God's kingdom: from a tiny seed, a plant will grow so large that birds will nest in it. Roosting birds are a biblical symbol for the nations of the earth.

The kingdom of God will be universal and people from every nationality will find rest in it.

The following Parable of Leaven represents the transformative power of God's kingdom. A small amount of leaven can change a large quantity of flour. Leaven works quietly and unseen, as Christ's influence works quietly in the hearts of believers. Leaven works from the inside out to produce a visible result. The kingdom of God works within God's people, the Church, to change the outside world, which will one day be completely healed from the corrupting influence of sin and Satan. That's worth shouting, "Hallelujah!"

REFLECT

Have you ever been annoyed by someone else's enthusiasm in a worship service? Why? Perhaps our negative reaction tells us more about ourselves than the other person. Where have you seen the kingdom of God working quietly, like leaven, to transform a person, a church, a family, or a community? Ask God to work within you to help change what's around you.

The Rev. Reagan W. Cocke

RESPOND

Day 19

THE NARROW DOOR / READ LUKE 13:22-30

> Let all the world in every corner sing
> My God and King.
> The heavens are not too high,
> His praise may thither fly:
> The earth is not too low,
> His praises there may grow.
> Let all the world in every corner sing
> My God and King.
> Let all the world in every corner sing
> My God and King.
> The Church with psalms must shout,
> No door can keep them out:
> But above all, the heart
> Must bear the longest part.
> Let all the world in every corner sing
> My God and King.[9]
>
> — George Herbert, 1593-1633

Who is within the kingdom of God? Who will be saved? Have you ever pondered these questions?

---

9. *The SPCK Book of Christian Prayer*, 22.

I've had many people ask me about loved ones and their salvation. I always ask first about the loved one's faith in Jesus. Often I discover the reason this person is asking is that they simply do not know about the person's faith in Christ.

Imagine how many years we can know each other and never have a conversation about Jesus. That should be astounding to people who claim to know and love Our Lord—that we do not speak to others about him, as if talking about him is taboo.

When I find a new restaurant I like, I always share it with others. Why would I want to keep it a secret? I want that place to thrive and be successful. I don't want it to be my personal restaurant. I could not sustain it by myself. And I want others to experience it. In the same way, talking about Jesus should be the most natural thing to do when we know him as master and friend.

In John 10:16 Jesus says, *"I have other sheep that are not of this fold. I must bring them also, and they will listen to my voice. So there will be one flock, one shepherd."* When we hear the voice of Jesus as our shepherd, we learn that he has plans for many more sheep, for a much greater party. And Jesus is clear that all who come to know and love him, these he calls to bring others to himself: *"Go therefore and make disciples of all nations…"* (Matthew 28:19).

Jesus also makes it clear there will be many surprises in the kingdom's membership. Hebrew writings of the day indicate that the rabbis believed all Israel would be saved except for some blatant sinners who excluded themselves. Jesus corrects that understanding by talking about a "narrow door." The door he is talking about is himself. Human history has narrowed down to *one person, in one place, at one time, for one event.* When Jesus of Nazareth is around thirty-three years old, he will die on a cross in Jerusalem for the sins of the world. The narrow door of salvation is through this one person—this God-man—the only One who can offer salvation.

The Episcopal and Anglican Holy Communion service includes "Comfortable Words" that explain who and what the narrow door is:

> *Come unto me, all ye that travail and are heavy laden, and I will refresh you.*
> — Matthew 11:28

> *God so loved the world, that he gave his only-begotten Son, to the end that all that believe in him should not perish, but have everlasting life.*
> —John 3:16

> *This is a true saying, and worthy of all men to be received, that Christ Jesus came into the world to save sinners.*
> —1 Timothy 1:15

> *If any man sin, we have an Advocate with the Father, Jesus Christ the righteous; and he is the perfect offering for our sins, and not for ours only, but for the sins of the whole world.*
> —1 John 2:1-2

To enter the narrow door, Jesus emphasizes people must "strive," which is a technical term for competing in the "Games" of his day. It denotes whole-hearted action. It does not mean that human achievement merits entrance; rather, it points to one's attitude. The many who are unable to enter are those who do not try to enter until it is too late.

The door may be narrow, but the invitation is to ALL to come and enter into new life in Jesus. While many believe that Jesus is somehow against sinners, the New Testament is clear that he is *for* sinners and welcomes all who come to him. Why would we not want to share this glorious message?

REFLECT

Who first told you about Jesus? Take a minute to thank God for them, and, if it is possible, reach out and thank them personally. If they are no longer alive, remember about the communion of saints and that one day you will be able to thank them (again) in person. Who can you share even a small thought about Jesus with this week?

The Rev. Reagan W. Cocke

RESPOND

_____
_____
_____
_____

Day 20

THE ROAD TO JERUSALEM / READ LUKE 13:31-35

Hardly any of us have been threatened with death or the prospect of death by a violent group or person.

Jesus was threatened with death almost from day one. Upon hearing of his birth from the magi following the star, Herod the Great sought to kill the young king. Warned by an angel in a dream, Joseph took Mary and Jesus to Egypt to protect his son. What an irony that Egypt, the nation that once threatened to destroy Israel, would become a place of refuge for Israel's Messiah, the Son of God, Jesus. Egypt is both a place of slavery and security in the history of God's people.

Similarly, the leaders of the people of God can either be a place of safety or slavery for God's people. When they listen to God and his leading, leaders of the faith protect the people of God. When they turn from God and his wisdom, they put the people in jeopardy. Jesus came to Israel to be the ultimate person of safety for God's people—their way of eternal salvation. At the close of his journey to Jerusalem and the Cross, Jesus will sacrificially become salvation—the Way, the Truth, and the Life—for the many.

But today's story takes place earlier, in Galilee, just as Jesus is beginning his journey to Jerusalem (Luke's travel narrative is based on theme, not chronology). Some Pharisees come to Jesus and encourage him to leave Galilee. Herod may have sent them to urge his departure so he would not have another John the Baptist disaster on his hands. (It was this Herod, initially enamored by the ministry of John, who imprisoned the Baptist when he confronted Herod about marrying his brother's wife.) After taking

John's life (his head on a platter) for a show of face at a party, Herod finds himself in another predicament—what to do about Jesus?

So Herod sends his people to Jesus, encouraging him to leave his jurisdiction. But Jesus will not be intimidated. He calls Herod a fox—a contemptuous expression meaning one who has no honor or majesty. Jesus says he will continue his ministry, suggesting Herod does have a chance to partake. But Jesus warns that his journey will soon come to an end; then it will be too late for Herod and his men. Jesus has one set purpose—to go to Jerusalem.

Unlike the other Gospel writers, Luke has a major emphasis on Jerusalem. The name Jerusalem is used ninety times in Luke's Gospel compared to only forty-nine times in the rest of the New Testament. As a writer to the Gentiles, Luke emphasizes Jerusalem to help non-Jews understand how important the city is in the purposes of God.

New Testament scholar Dr. Leon Morris writes, "It was at Jerusalem, before the Sanhedrin, that trials of prophets took place. It was there that the nation's attitude to Jesus would take its final shape and that death take place that would accomplish God's purpose for his Messiah."[10] In saying *"How often would I have gathered your children…"* (13:34), Jesus indicates, as we find in John's Gospel, that he went to Jerusalem several times during his ministry and not just the one time mentioned in the Synoptic Gospels (Matthew, Mark, and Luke).

In the final verse of today's passage, Jesus quotes from Psalm 118:26, which says, *"Blessed is he who comes in the name of the Lord!"* (13:35). As Galilean pilgrims entered Jerusalem annually for Passover, they would chorus this psalm. And, this is what the crowds will soon shout when Jesus enters the city on Palm Sunday. But Jesus' meaning here is most likely a reference

---

10. Morris, *Luke: An Introduction*, 250.

to his second coming, when he will finally draw from Jerusalem recognition as the Messiah, however unwilling it comes from the city that will have rejected and killed him.

REFLECT

Many in our culture reject Jesus and his identity as the Messiah. What do you think about that rejection? How do you respond? Jesus kept firm to his one purpose—to go to Jerusalem and the Cross. Where do you need help in keeping firm to your purpose to follow him on The Disciple's Way?

The Rev. Reagan W. Cocke

RESPOND

_____

_____

_____

_____

Day 21

RESISTANCE TO THE GOOD / READ LUKE 14:1-6

Have you ever resisted a good thing?

Today's passage and the next two passages (verses 7-14 and 15-24) all occur at the same dinner. In Jesus' day, meals were pivotal social functions for sharing, celebrating, and connecting with those of your same status. Meals were used to reinforce social hierarchy. These first three encounters in Luke 14 take place in the home of a Pharisee, with other powerful and influential religious leaders present. It is the Sabbath day.

In the Gospels, there are seven occasions when Jesus heals someone on a Sabbath day. One might think that so many miracles would have made the healer a respected and beloved individual. Unfortunately, as we know, this was not the case. Jesus' amazing healings (and the accompanying teachings during these episodes) only made the religious authorities more suspect and resentful of him. Today's story as a whole is enveloped in hostility.

I've often wondered how Jesus came to be invited to dinners such as these, considering how much opposition he was encountering from the very people with whom he was dining. Perhaps an even more puzzling question is why a man with dropsy was at the dinner. Today this ailment is more commonly known as "edema," or swelling due to water retention. In biblical times, people with this affliction were often regarded as unclean. I think it is entirely possible this man was planted at the dinner by the Pharisees to test Jesus, especially in light of Luke's telling us that Jesus was being carefully watched.

Jesus was under scrutiny. When we feel scrutinized, most of us become anxious. Not so with Jesus. One thing we see in this story, and repeatedly in the Gospels, is the peace Jesus brings to such hostile encounters. In addition to a sense of peace, Jesus also brings a different set of rules. The Gospels continually show us that Jesus crosses conventional boundaries; he includes the "wrong people" and he generally departs from the accepted norms. Jesus has a distinctive viewpoint on the world—God's viewpoint.

Several observations can be made about this encounter. First, Jesus again takes the role of authoritative teacher who declares what is acceptable on the Sabbath. Second, the silence of the leadership indicates their perplexity and inability to effectively counter Jesus' message and actions—they are, once more, outwitted. Third, the God of all does not cease to be kind, good, and loving to those in need. Finally, Luke connects healing with freedom and release (see verse 4). The man is sent on his way. Healings of all kinds include release.

Our Lord challenged the social world of his day to accept his invitation to participate in God's redemptive work. It was the ultimate invitation to see the world in a different way, to help bring about the kingdom of God here on earth. They Pharisees missed it or, more accurately, they actively resisted it. I once heard a definition of sin as "resistance to Jesus." Here we see resistance clearly. Where do you see this resistance in today's world?

REFLECT

In this account, we have a clear example of resistance to Jesus. Resistance is not always so easily observed. In your own life, consider your "resistance to Jesus" in the broadest sense. What causes such resistance for you, and how will you commit to a more conscious life of discipleship, celebrating the redemptive work of God?

The Rt. Rev. Gary Lillibridge

RESPOND

_____

_____

_____

_____

Week Four

ETERNAL FELLOWSHIP

He said also to the man who had invited him, "When you give a dinner or a banquet, do not invite your friends or your brothers or your relatives or rich neighbors, lest they also invite you in return and you be repaid. But when you give a feast, invite the poor, the crippled, the lame, the blind, and you will be blessed, because they cannot repay you. For you will be repaid at the resurrection of the just."

LUKE 14:12-14

CONSIDER

Are you seeking friendships that will give you earthly advantage or eternal treasure?

Day 22

HUMILITY AND HONOR / READ LUKE 14:7-14

One of the common settings for philosophical discussions in Greek culture was a banquet.

Eating and drinking together provided a context for some serious and some frivolous discussions about life. In ancient Greece, a drinking party often followed a meal and was known as a "symposium" —combining "pinein" (to drink) with "syn" (together). The motivation of these symposiums was often drinking over thinking. Much later, this term came to be used to define gatherings of an intellectual sort with more emphasis on ideas than imbibing—at least usually!

In yesterday's devotion, I noted that Jesus had once again established his authority as a teacher in stumping the Pharisees with his question about healing on the Sabbath. Having done this, he now turns to everyone present at the banquet to address them directly on the subject of humility and honor. The scene Luke portrays for us is a somber one, tension filling the air.

There are two parts of Jesus' remarks here: verses 7-11 and verses 12-14. Although they address different subjects, the parts are closely related. Luke uses parallel language to present the teachings: Jesus **addresses** his fellow guests (v.7) and then **addresses** his host (v.12). Jesus mentions the receiving of **invitations** (v.8) and then the responsibilities of **hosting** (v.12). There are two **"do nots…"** (vs.8, 12) followed by two **"But whens…"** (vs.10, 13). Finally, Luke uses two *"you will be's…"* (vs.10, 14).

As Jesus takes on the subjects of honor and humility, he is certainly not a forerunner of the modern "Miss Manners." In fact, he completely reverses the constructs of the society he is in, proposing new and shocking alternatives. He warns against self-importance and pride,

At first glance, it might appear that in the first section Jesus is simply reinforcing the accepted wisdom of the ancient world. Proverbs 25:6-7 states, *"Do not put yourself forward in the king's presence or stand in the place of the great, for it is better to be told, 'Come up here,' than to be put lower in the presence of a noble."* If we quit reading the story at verse 11, Jesus' remarks could be viewed simply as a reminder of this familiar advice. But when we come to verse 11, we see the parable at work on the deepest of levels: *"For everyone who exalts himself will be humbled, and he who humbles himself will be exalted"* (14:11). Be exalted by whom? Jesus' is about to make it clear.

This second part (vs.12-14) of his teaching is even more shocking. Jesus suggests that it is better to invite the lame, crippled, and poor to your banquet than your rich friends and relatives, who can repay you. Imagine such words falling on the ears of those who carefully hand-picked their dinner guests to reinforce their status at the top of society. Yet it's clear Jesus expects his hearers to take his words literally. In verse 14, he shares the happy reward for such honoring of the lowly: *"...you will be blessed...you will be repaid at the resurrection of the just."* Jesus makes it clear that choosing humility is not just a wise move socially; it is choosing to live God's way, to reflect the very heart of God in your attitudes and your behavior. And, as a result, it is God himself who will exalt you on the last day.

This teaching is consistent with the theme of divine reversal Luke highlights from the beginning. Consider Mary's Song in Luke 1:52-53, *"...he has brought down the mighty from their thrones and exalted those of humble estate; he has filled the hungry with good things, and the rich he has sent away empty."* In the Gospel of John, we find another example of the blessed humility of a disciple when John the Baptist states, *"He (Jesus) must increase, but I must decrease"* (John 3:30).

Jesus' teaching in today's passage was not just for everyone present at the banquet that day. Jesus is also speaking to all of us, in our own day, regardless of whether we play the role of guest or host. It is the attitude of the heart the Lord is concerned about. The Disciple's Way is one of humility, not only in relation to others, but especially as it relates to our position in the sight of God.

REFLECT

In our own day, and in your life in particular, how do customs and status impede your ability to reach out to others? If you were to take Jesus' advice literally and host a dinner for the poor, the crippled, and others in need, where would you begin? What is stopping you? Is there a place in your life where you need to embrace the humility of a disciple? Ask God to help you today.

The Rt. Rev. Gary Lillibridge

RESPOND

Day 23

GUEST LISTS / READ LUKE 14:15-24

Jesus' dinner at the home of the Pharisee continues.

At this point in the narrative, Jesus invokes one of the primary metaphors of Jewish eschatological thought—the heavenly banquet. To further make his point about the new order of God's kingdom, Jesus tells the story about the rejection of a host by his peers and the subsequent unusual list of invitees, which includes the poor and the needy. The parable Jesus tells represents a stark contrast to the social system of peer-to-peer dinners in his day, based on one's standing in society.

Jesus refers to customs of the day that would have been well known to his audience.

In Palestine, when someone was planning a party/feast/banquet, the event was announced well in advance. Guests would need time to decide if they were going, based on who else was invited (since meals such as these helped to secure one's status in the community). The exact time of the banquet was not included in the initial "save the date" announcement. Rather, when everything was ready on the day of the feast, servants were sent out to those who had replied with an affirmative "RSVP" to let them know the party was about to begin. To say "yes" and then back out after preparations had been made was a great insult, for animals had to be killed and crops harvested in proportion to the number of people expected. Much hard work had been invested by the host before the party even began.

Many commentators on this passage cite Deuteronomy 20:5-7 as a source for the excuses offered by those who originally said "yes" but then backed out at the last minute. Although it is not an exact fit, it is close enough for Jesus to have had this passage in mind as either irony or a joke at the expense of his hearers. As religious leaders schooled in the Scriptures, they would certainly have known the reference.

In the Deuteronomy passage, three situations are listed as acceptable for someone to be excused from war. Since this is not war, but rather a wonderful party, Jesus might be using the Deuteronomy passage to underscore the seeming outlandishness of the excuses given in his parable (buying a field, buying oxen, recent marriage). In any case, the excuses offered are all focused on the guests' self-interests. Remember who Jesus is talking to here. The would-be guests were those preoccupied with possessions and status. These are people who have not embraced the values that flow from a deep commitment to God whose *"good pleasure"* it is to *"give you the Kingdom"* (Luke 12:32).

As the story unfolds, the point seems to be that adopting a new set of social values means the host will include anyone among his table guests who accepts his invitation. In the spiritual parallel, all kinds of people, regardless of social status, who accept God's generous invitation to join him shall indeed feast with him.

What about those invited at the end of the parable? Verse 23 reads, *"And the master said to the servant, 'Go out to the highways and hedges and compel people to come in, that my house may be filled."* (Unfortunately, some Christians throughout the ages have used the word "compel" here to justify forcing people to become Christians, including by violence if deemed necessary. Many religious wars have been waged on this misunderstood verse, resulting in inexcusable cruelty.)

What Jesus means is that it is necessary to "compel" this third group of invitees to come to the banquet because they would not be inclined to accept this invitation on first pass *since their social status did not allow it.* They were not able to reciprocate on the level such an invitation would require. They belonged to an altogether different social world. One simply did not cross such boundaries. In short, they would feel unworthy because society had told them they were unworthy.

Per usual, Jesus reverses this flawed value system. As the entirety of the first twenty-four verses of Luke 14 clearly indicate, God doesn't invite people to his heavenly banquet (eternal life) based on their social status, what they can offer him, or what the world thinks of them. God's invitation is based solely on his great, great love for sinners. Thanks be to God!

REFLECT

God's heavenly banquet is not just for the future; it is beginning now. As disciples of Jesus, we are to be about the work of inviting people in, and participating in, God's grand feast of activity. What in your life can you release (practices, pursuits, attitudes, etc.) and what can you take into your life more fully so as to RSVP "Yes" to God's invitation to participate in the celebration of his kingdom here and now?

The Rt. Rev. Gary Lillibridge

RESPOND

_____

_____

_____

_____

Day 24

THE COST OF DISCIPLESHIP / READ LUKE 14:25-35

Jesus continues on his way to Jerusalem.

After his healing and teaching in the previous sections of Luke 14 (during dinner at the home of the Pharisee), Jesus knows trouble is ahead. He also knows that his followers will be in for a difficult and demanding life, even after he is no longer with them. Careful, thoughtful preparation of mind and spirit is necessary for those who shall pick up their cross and follow him.

Jesus must not have had any political consultants, because he's definitely not saying the things that attract people to a cause! Specifically, hating your family and your own life, as well as forfeiting your possessions, are not the kind of recruitment slogans that draw the masses.

Anglican theologian N. T. Wright, in his commentary on this passage, encourages us to see Jesus' exhortations as the necessary commitments for embarking on a great expedition rather than carefully crafted words to increase one's popularity. He notes that if you are on a mission to bring urgent medical care to villagers in a remote area (or any dangerous work), necessity requires leaving some things behind. The path might be too steep to carry everything. The mission may be dangerous—hence, be prepared. It's possible some of the party may not make it back to their families.[11] Granted, we may not like the sound of these things, but in the context of a great expedition, Jesus' comments make sense.

---

11. N. T. Wright, *Luke for Everyone* (Louisville, KY: Westminster John Knox Press, 2004), 180.

Christianity espouses many values as part of an authentic, godly life, and these include the value of family. It can be shocking to hear Jesus say that we will need to hate our family. But, of course, Jesus is speaking in comparative terms, saying that all other loves and concerns must take a back seat to the high calling of discipleship when helping to bring about the Kingdom of God. In effect, Jesus is saying, "Think about what this will cost you; and cost you it will." Andrew, Peter, James, and John learned this hard yet blessed truth after accepting Jesus' invitation to become fishers of people.

I believe the call to The Disciple's Way needs to be considered in the same way a couple considers taking marriage vows. They weigh the words of the priest carefully, that marriage is not to be entered into lightly or unadvisedly, but deliberately and reverently. This is very good advice when committing one's self to Jesus as well; for it is one thing to admire Jesus, it is quite another to become a disciple.

I am reminded of the story of an esteemed professor who was talking with a colleague who remarked, "(So-and-so) tells me he was one of your students." The professor responded, "He may have attended my lectures, but he was not one of my students." In the same vein, it is possible to follow Jesus at a distance without being a disciple. Not only is this possible, it is all too common.

In today's reading, Jesus is using vivid language to call for the reconstruction of one's very identity, based not on family or societal connections, but on the call of being his disciple. It is important to Jesus that the crowd around him that day, as well as we ourselves, grasp the deep meaning and ongoing repercussions of the call of Jesus—and count the cost before signing up.

Let us acknowledge that Christian discipleship is a dynamic and life-long journey. In the words of Gregory of Nyssa, "One stone does not make a complete tower, nor does one commandment bring the perfection of the soul to its desired measure."[12] One must lay a foundation and then build upon it with precious stones. In the words of St. Paul, *"Now if anyone builds on the foundation (of Jesus) with gold, silver, precious stones, wood, hay, straw, each one's work will become manifest..."* (1 Corinthians 3:12-13). Are you ready to build your life upon the cornerstone of Jesus? To become his disciple?

REFLECT

Today's devotion is rich with imagery. Which of the following images stand out for you and why: family connections, carrying your cross, building a tower with a strong foundation, military strategy, precious stones, or saltiness? How do the words of Jesus in this passage encourage your discipleship? Help you take it more seriously?

The Rt. Rev. Gary Lillibridge

RESPOND

---

12. Arthur A. Just, Jr., Ed., *Ancient Christian Commentary on Scripture, Luke* (Downers Grove, Illinois: InterVarsity Press, 2003), 242.

Day 25

TROUBLESOME COMPANIONS / READ LUKE 15:1-2

Some have called the 15th chapter of St. Luke "the gospel within the gospel."

This chapter contains three parables that represent the very essence of the Good News. These three parables are similar in that they all include: 1) someone who loses something, 2) the loss recovered, 3) a restoration, and 4) a concluding celebration.

Here, we once again see Jesus extending to his critics an invitation to join him in the loving, merciful, reconciling work of God. Each of the parables he tells provides deep insight into God's disposition regarding sinners. In the two devotions following this one, we will look at each of these parables individually. But today we focus on the first two verses which introduce them.

These opening two sentences set the framework for the entire 15th chapter. Luke states that the tax collectors and sinners were all *"drawing near to hear [Jesus]"* (15:1). This verse is connected to the previous verse, which ends chapter 14, in which Jesus says, *"He who has ears to hear, let him hear."* (Chapter divisions were added later.) In other words, who has ears to hear? The tax collectors and sinners!

Going back to the beginning of Luke, the first four verses of his book (Luke 1:1-4, read them) provide important clues about Luke's writing. Luke is addressing Theophilus, which could be a person or persons, since the name is often translated "lover of God." Why would Theophilus need another version of the teaching he's already heard? Luke's answer is that his own purpose is to provide an *"orderly account"* so that the reader might *"have certainty concerning the things you have been taught"* (1:4). Therefore, his audience is a Christian one or, at a minimum, includes early Christians. Luke also has a major emphasis in his entire Gospel on prophecy and fulfillment, hence his opening statement in verse 1 which says, *"the things that have been accomplished (fulfilled) among us."* (Luke 1:1)

Luke's "order" is often a connection of theme, not sequence. We see Luke's orderly account come into play in today's verses (15:1-2) as he connects them with the end of chapter 14 with the theme of "hearing." As this chapter begins, we witness a drawing near to "hear" Jesus. We also see quite the cast of characters assembled here, including tax collectors, so-called sinners, Pharisees, and scribes. Luke often talks about "lawyers" in tandem with Pharisees; at other times, he uses the word "scribes," which was the more common description of this group at the time. (The lawyers/scribes had knowledge of the law and could draft legal documents.)

As it turns out, it seems the tax collectors and sinners were the ones who actually had "ears to hear" Jesus, while the Pharisees and scribes continued to grumble about him. This reminds me of the grumbling of the Israelites wandering through the desert with Moses. I wonder why so many religious people find reason to grumble when there is so much to celebrate about God's expansive love for us.

But the Pharisees did not like that God's love was extending through Jesus to groups they considered inferior: *"This man receives sinners and eats with them"* (15:2). This seems to be the Achilles' heel of the religious elite of Jesus' day—an inability to see themselves for who they really were, sinners in need of a Savior.

Luke's audience would likely have heard all kinds of information about Jesus and this new movement before now. But Luke uses the phrase "among us" in verse 1, bringing the story to their present day. In other words, the Word was alive and well among them. They were now encountering Jesus and his work for themselves. Would they have "ears to hear?"

REFLECT

Today's two introductory verses may seem simple, but they have great richness and depth. Take an honest look at your own attitudes. Do you live in ways that celebrate the goodness of God? Or do you find yourself grumbling much of the time? The Word is alive and well in our day, just as it was in Luke's. How easy is it for you to really "hear" Jesus? What gets in the way?

The Rt. Rev. Gary Lillibridge

RESPOND

_____

_____

_____

_____

Day 26

CELEBRATING THE RECOVERY OF THE LOST /
READ LUKE 15:3-10

Today's two parables are strong on their own merits, yet they also serve as a "warm-up" to the longer parable of the lost son, which we will discuss tomorrow.

In the first parable, the shepherd not only finds the lost sheep, but places it upon his shoulders and heads homeward. With this one small detail, Luke paints a touching picture of God—the shepherd who gently rescues his sheep. We also hear hints of the voice of the prophet Ezekiel (34:1-24) who chastises the shepherds of Israel for disregarding God's people. Ezekiel quotes God as saying, *"For thus says the Lord God: Behold, I, I myself will search for my sheep and will seek them out...And I will set up over them one shepherd, my servant David, and he shall feed them: he shall feed them and be their shepherd"* (34:11, 23).

It was not out of the ordinary in ancient Israel for a shepherd to encounter circumstances that would require him to risk, or even lay down, his life for his sheep. The flocks of Israel at times belonged to individuals, but many times they were communal flocks. In other words, a flock or flocks belonged to an entire village. In these cases, there would be two or three shepherds assigned to care for the flocks.

At the end of the day, the shepherds whose flocks were all safely together would return to the village. In the event one or more of the sheep had gone missing, the village would be informed that one of the shepherds had remained behind to go out and look for it. The village would be on watch;

when they saw the shepherd returning, a shout of thanksgiving and welcome would ring out from the villagers. It doesn't take a vivid imagination to see why Jesus referred to this custom in his parable about the love of God: *"For the Son of man came to seek and to save the lost"* (Luke 19:10).

When I am preaching on the Resurrection, I like to say, "You should be careful out there, because Jesus is on the loose and he is looking for you." The risen Christ is a seeking Christ, a pursuing Christ. Another image I find meaningful is found in the words of St. Ambrose, in his commentary on today's passage, "The shoulders of Christ (carrying the sheep) are the arms of the cross."[13]

As we turn now to the second story in this section, notice that it is a practice of Luke to include both female and male examples in making his points:

Zechariah and Elizabeth (chapter 1), Simeon and Hannah (chapter 2), Elijah and the widow at Zarephath (chapter 4), Simon and his mother-in-law (also chapter 4), the widow from Nain and her son (chapter 7), the Pharisee and the woman who anoints Jesus (also Chapter 7), and the list goes on. It is also characteristic of Luke to reference possessions in some way; for example, a coin is central to this story. One special meaning for me is found in the statement that the woman lit a lamp to look for the coin. It was only by the "light" that she was able to recover what had been lost. For those with "ears to hear," think about what that means.

These two parables are arranged in similar ways; namely, losing something, searching for it, finding it, and calling friends and neighbors to celebrate. The elements in both these stories (and the one tomorrow) certainly provide the impetus for a verse of the hymn, "There's a Wideness in God's Mercy," which states "For the love of God is broader than the

---

13. Arthur A. Just, Jr., Ed., *Ancient Christian Commentary*, 244.

measure of the mind; And the heart of the Eternal is most wonderfully kind."[14]

At the end of each of these parables, Jesus drives home the spiritual point:

"Just so, I tell you, there will be more joy in heaven over one sinner who repents than over ninety-nine righteous persons who need no repentance" (15:7). And, *"I tell you, there is joy before the angels of God over one sinner who repents"* (15:10).

It is as if all of heaven is having a party in these parables! We know that the kingdom of God extends to heaven and to earth. We, too, ought to rejoice with the heavens over one sinner who comes to repentance. This is the disciple's heart.

REFLECT

In the Lord's Prayer, we pray, "Thy kingdom come, thy will be done, on earth as it is in heaven." What are some examples for you of God's will on earth? What might you do to help foster the kingdom of heaven on earth this week in your following of Jesus, the Great Shepherd of the sheep?

The Rt. Rev. Gary Lillibridge

RESPOND

___

14. Episcopal Hymnal, 1982, Hymn #470.

Day 27

THE VALUE OF MERCY / READ LUKE 15:11-32

The Parable of the Prodigal Son, as it is popularly known, is one of the greatest short stories in the world.

It has been memorialized by writers and artists down through the ages. Many of its terms are still in use. The phrase "kill the fatted calf" is a metaphor for a festive celebration. The word "prodigal," though sometimes used to mean "to return home," actually means wasteful, excessive, irresponsible, self-indulgent, imprudent, and other terms of self-centeredness. In Jesus' story, the self-indulgent son does in fact return home to a loving and merciful welcome (at least by the father), hence the common usage of "returning." Of course, Jesus did not title the parables—we did. So while the title "The Parable of the Prodigal Son" does fit, this story could equally be called "The Parable of the Loving Father" or even "The Parable of the Hardhearted Son."

Whatever label we give it, this story has meaning on so many levels that each of us should find a way to relate to one or more of the characters involved.

Jesus' parable is divided into three main elements. One focuses on the younger son's "coming to himself." A second focuses on the mercy of the father. The third focuses on the resentment of the older son. Let us look briefly at each.

First, the younger son asked for his inheritance early. He makes this request with a rather callous attitude, which seems to be something along the lines of, "I'll get it one day anyway, so give it to me now." After wasting his entire inheritance, Jesus notes that the son came to his senses or, even better, *"he came to himself"* (15:17). Really, what could be "farther away" than departing from one's self? Winston Churchill, in his book *A Far Country*, notes that the true alien land for a person is the loss of their standards and ideals.[15] This younger son only comes back to his true self on the way home. The point Jesus is making is that home is in God's loving embrace.

Secondly, the father shows sweet mercy. Our parents, and we who are parents, know the angst of letting a child learn the hard way. This father understood that both his child and the inheritance might be lost in a dangerous and hostile world. Yet, this is a risk he was willing to take. When he eventually sees his son returning home, the father does not wait for him to arrive at the front door. He rushes out to greet him, embracing and kissing him! Certainly not the welcome the younger son expected, I am sure. His surprise and delight become our surprise and delight at the grace of God as described by Jesus. It reminds me of the beautiful words found in Psalm 85:10, *"Steadfast love and faithfulness meet; righteousness and peace kiss each other."*

On some level, one might wish the parable ended here, at verse 24, before we see the older son's response to his brother's return. Yet this part of the parable is absolutely essential to Jesus' full-orbed story about the nature of humanity, which all too often fails to celebrate that which ought to be celebrated.

The elder son is a "prodigal" of a different kind—he was as distant in spirit as his brother was in body. When speaking to his father about all that had happened, the older son doesn't even refer to his little brother as brother, but rather calls him *"this son of yours"* (15:30). The father gently corrects him in verse 32 by saying *"this your brother."* The rivalry here reminds me of the Cain and Abel story in Genesis in which Cain asks God,

---

15. *The Interpreter's Bible*, vol. 8, (Nashville: John Abingdon Press, 1978), 270.

"*Am I my brother's keeper?*" God responds, in so many words, "As a matter of fact, you are."

So, we have a story about a father who is drawn into the complexities of his children. Most of us can relate, either as a parent or as those who have had parents (and may understand their challenges a bit better now that we are adults). Being people with "feet of clay" (faulted), we all know the need of mercy. The father's mercy in this story represents Jesus' prophetic message of God's desire to draw all people "home" to himself.

REFLECT

Did your parents allow you to learn things the hard way or rescue you from difficulty? If you are a parent, how easy is it for you to refrain from interfering when your child needs to learn a lesson? When is it appropriate to step in to help those we love? Think about a time someone close to you did something hurtful or foolish. How easy was it for you to extend mercy and forgiveness?

The Rt. Rev. Gary Lillibridge

RESPOND

Day 28

WHAT SHALL I DO? / READ LUKE 16:1-9

We face the question *"What shall I do?"* in many situations of our everyday lives.

Luke uses this question in today's text (16:3). Furthermore, he includes this same question in a number of his stories. It is uttered by the rich fool (12:17-18). The crowds ask John the Baptist the question (3:10-14). nd, after his sermon in Acts 2, Peter is presented with the same question by his hearers (Acts 2:37). In times of confusion, challenge, or crisis, biblical stories often include this phrase.

As chapter 15 gives way to chapter 16, we have a change in audience. Whereas chapter 15 is primarily directed to the Pharisees and scribes, the audience in chapter 16 is Jesus' disciples.

Though the audiences differ, the previous story of the Prodigal Son (Chapter 15) and today's story of the Shrewd Manager have similarities. In both stories, the central character faces a crisis created by his own mismanagement of property or possessions. This irresponsibility creates a crisis for the character. As a result, each has a critical choice to make. Therefore the question, *"What shall I do?"* comes to the fore in both stories.

Jesus' parable of the Shrewd Manager, read on a surface level, is surely one of his most confusing. Considering the perplexing nature of the story, we might be asking ourselves, *"What shall we do"* with this teaching?

Theologian Joel B. Green notes in his commentary that this story is not an allegory in the same sense as most of Jesus' parables. In Jesus' other parables, there are usually more obvious references to God and/or Jesus within the story. But in this parable, Jesus is using an example from everyday life, from cultural suppositions, to comment on the way the world often works.[16]

We read this story and perhaps think, "How could such dishonesty be a trait that Jesus seems to commend?" Fundamental to understanding the story is to see that what is actually going on here. The shrewd manager is being commended for using money (mammon) to secure a place for himself, not for his dishonesty. Jesus tells his disciples (v.8) that they need to be as creative and shrewd with the treasure they've been entrusted (the Good News) as others in the world are with something that has no lasting power—mammon/money/wealth.

Sometimes it can be helpful to look back and consider how the Church fathers and scholars who have gone before us have interpreted a passage. Below are three thoughts paraphrased from some of the ancient writers about this story. Read them over and consider why and how one or more of them speak to you:

St. Augustine: Jesus is recommending to the disciples the shrewd manager's foresight, prudence, and ingenuity.[17]

Ephrem the Syrian: By using the transitory things of this world which are not ours, we are to purchase for ourselves those things which will not pass away.[18]

John Chrysostom: Riches are a loan from God that are to be deposited with

---

16. Joel B. Green, *The Gospel of Luke* (Grand Rapids: William B. Eerdmans Publishing Company, 1997), p. 589.

17. Arthur A. Just, Jr., Ed., *Ancient Christian Commentary on Scripture, Luke* (Downers Grove, Illinois: InterVarsity Press, 2003), 254.

18. Just, Jr., *Ancient Christian Commentary*, p. 254.

the poor so that we might receive a hundredfold reward, for they will be our friends in the eternal habitations.[19]

As noted in the final two thoughts above, this parable is often understood to emphasize almsgiving as vitally important to the Christian life. Jesus says that using one's resources in a selfless and generous manner has eternal rewards (v.9). Earthly goods, wonderful as they may be, do not endure. As we will see in the next reflection, being trustworthy with worldly wealth surely means, from God's point of view, being generous with it and giving it away (v.11).

REFLECT

I titled this meditation, "What shall I do?" because of Luke's frequent use of the question when someone is faced with a challenge. Specifically then, "What shall you do" with today's teaching from Jesus in your own discipleship? "What shall you do" with the resources you've been given as you faithfully live out the call of Jesus?

The Rt. Rev. Gary Lillibridge

RESPOND

_____

_____

_____

_____

19. Ibid.

Week Five

GENEROUS SERVICE

One who is faithful in a very little is also faithful in much, and one who is dishonest in a very little is also dishonest in much. If then you have not been faithful in the unrighteous wealth, who will entrust to you the true riches? And if you have not been faithful in that which is another's, who will give you that which is your own? No servant can serve two masters, for either he will hate the one and love the other, or he will be devoted to the one and despise the other. You cannot serve God and money.

LUKE 16:10-13

CONSIDER

Will you steward the blessings God has given you with grateful generosity?

Day 29

WHICH MASTER WILL YOU SERVE? / READ LUKE 16:10-13

Are we less concerned with eternal treasures than with earthly possessions?

In today's teaching, Jesus expands his comments on the themes introduced in verses 1-9 in the parable of the Shrewd Manager. That challenging story provides the background for the four verses we now consider. In the Shrewd Manager parable, we learned that we ought to use our earthly possessions in a way that helps secure eternal treasures and heavenly rewards. As we turn to verses 10-13, we will now learn that clinging to possessions as the ultimate value of life leads to separation from God.

The 16th century theologian and pastor John Calvin, in his commentary on these verses, noted that it was fruitless to try to interpret each verse in detail; to do so is to miss Jesus' central points. He observed that one particular point Christ is making here is that the children of the present age are far more diligent (shrewd) with regard to their own fleeting interests than the children of the light are with regard to their eternal well-being (vs.8-9).

In considering how one might be more diligent or shrewd with our earthly wealth and with the Good News in particular, Jesus presents a series of contrasts: honest vs. dishonest (v.10); faithful vs. not faithful (v.10); little vs. much (v.10); dishonest wealth vs. true riches (v.11); riches of others vs. riches of your own (v.12); two different masters (v.13); hate vs. love (v.13); and devotion vs. despising (v.13). This dual approach to values shapes the text as we are presented with the choice between something lesser and something greater.

Once Jesus identifies the "masters" (God, money), it becomes clear that it's impossible to serve both. Dual service to these masters will always lead to conflicted interest, for they have contrary wills and opposing mindsets. When money becomes an idol, it encourages pride, greed, and the acquisition of power. God, on the other hand, calls his followers to humility, generosity, and servanthood. As the old saying goes, "Money is a great servant, but a terrible master." How true that is. Time and again, preoccupation with money and wealth result in 'mammon' becoming our lord and master. But, be sure, money/wealth is not evil in and of itself. It is simply a "thing."

Few virtues have the ability to serve God's purposes more effectively than generosity, whether it is of time, energy, or financial resources. An orientation in one's life to God as "master" and wealth as "servant" has always done, and continues to do, great things. The needs and the possibilities are endless. All it takes to put this dynamic into motion is to open our hearts to those in need.

When real generosity becomes the mark of a person's life and attitudes, money can be transformed into a useful servant in helping to accomplish the kingdom's goals. But God-like generosity includes more than money; it encompasses the use of our time, energy, and skill set in the service of our Lord. It extends to the whole way we see the world—and most importantly—the people in the world. There is plenty of need in our world. Generous hearts see it and follow Jesus' example in responding to those needs. This is a significant part of what it means to follow Jesus on The Disciple's Way.

The key to this whole first section of Luke 16 is steadfast faithfulness to God in all segments of our lives; for God's dominion is not limited, but arches over all—including our possessions. This faithfulness is rooted in our first loving God, who first loved us, and from that love, loving our neighbor and therein sharing in Christ's redeeming work.

REFLECT

What "masters" in your life would be better positioned as "servants"? What will it take to change those rankings in your life? How has God called you to use your wealth (money, time, energy, skills) to serve those around you? Ask God to give you eyes to see the need and a generous heart to follow your Savior in reaching out to the poor and hurting around you.

The Rt. Rev. Gary Lillibridge

RESPOND

_____

_____

_____

_____

Day 30

SINS OF OMISSION / READ LUKE 16:14-31

Who or what are we *not* seeing that is right in front of us?

This portion of Luke 16 has three sections: four verses on the law and the kingdom of God, including a comment on the true hearts of the Pharisees (vs.14-17); one verse on divorce and adultery in response to the lax approach to faithfulness in Jesus' day (v.18); and thirteen verses that tell the main story in this section, that of the rich man and Lazarus (vs.19-31).

What we have here is yet another lesson from Jesus about how his followers should conduct themselves. We are told in verse 15 that God *"knows (the Pharisees') hearts."* Because their hearts were not centered on God's way of being in the world, neither did they live out God's will. This connection between "seeing" God's way with our hearts and "doing" God's will with our actions is the dominant theme of Jesus' next parable: the rich man and Lazarus.

Let me say at the outset that the Lazarus mentioned in this parable is not to be confused with Mary and Martha's brother of the same name who Jesus raised from the dead in John's Gospel. In addition, this is the only one of Jesus' parables in which one of the characters (Lazarus) is given a name. The name Lazarus is a form of the name Eleazar which means "God is my help." Jesus does not give a name to the rich man in the parable; however, over the years he has acquired the symbolic name "Dives" (the Latin word for "rich").

The Parable of the Rich Man and Lazarus speaks for itself and, like all great stories, each individual line is critical to the parable as a whole. Read it thoroughly.

One of the things we should not overlook is that Lazarus is quite literally the rich man Dives' *neighbor*. He is right at his gate (his neighborhood). We know what Jesus said about neighbors—we are to love them. As this story unfolds, we learn that Dives is about as cold-hearted as they come, both in this life and the next. But what, really, was Dives' sin? Apparently, he had not ordered Lazarus to be removed from his gate. It does not appear that Dives was actively cruel to him, like pushing or kicking him when he passed. There is no indication that Dives forbade Lazarus from having the crumbs which the dogs often received.

Dives' ultimate sin, then, was that he never really *saw* Lazarus. This poor man was simply part of the landscape of the neighborhood. Dives' sin, then, was one of omission, not commission. Scottish Bible Commentator William Barclay, in his commentary on this passage, says that it was not what Dives *did* that got him into hell; it was what he *did not* do.[20] And then the great irony in the parable: Dives had never lifted a finger on earth to help Lazarus; yet while in Hades, Dives appeals to Abraham to have Lazarus dip his finger in water to cool his tongue for him. Talk about gall.

Dives makes me angry—until I realize that, on too many occasions, I am just like him. A few years ago I decided I was not going to act like Dives anymore. I cannot say I have perfected this change, but God continues to nudge me along, actively pushing me out of my comfort zone. In the dangerous world in which we live, reaching out to the needy requires paying attention to Jesus' admonition to be wise as serpents yet gentle/innocent as doves. To be careful is to be smart; but just because a situation may be

---

20. William Barclay, *The Gospel of Luke* (Philadelphia: The Westminster Press, 1956), p. 222.

a bit risky doesn't mean God isn't calling us to do something about it or within it.

Here's one example. I'm usually hesitant to give cash to someone on the street who is soliciting money from passersby. This is because, after many years in ministry, I've seen first-hand that many people use the money to support an addiction of one sort or another. But I still want to feed the hungry and give drink to the thirsty.

In response, I now carry several lunch bags in my car with water bottles, non-perishable and easy-to-open food, plastic utensils, and so forth. If I am not in my car, and there is a food establishment nearby, I often walk with the person in need and pay for his/her meal. I may not be solving world hunger, but one person is receiving some nourishment along the way. And I believe that I am being shaped more into the ways of Jesus on these occasions by not channeling my inner-Dives (namely, ignoring a need right in front of me).

Just becoming conscious of what is around us and making small gestures in response helps orient our hearts toward God's very heart. Interestingly, my lunch-bag practice has led to an increase in my participation (financially, prayerfully, hands-on, board service, etc.) with organizations that are doing more for our neighbors than I could do as one person.

Part of following Jesus on The Disciple's Way is loving our neighbor. But we can't really love our neighbor until we really *see* our neighbor, which was the problem in Dives' life. Let's pray for eyes to see and hearts to respond.

REFLECT

Dives did not really "see" Lazarus, though he was right in front of him. Are there needs you are not seeing, though they are close around you? Take a minute to consider. Then ask God to open your eyes to what you may never have noticed before. How can you respond in the ways of Jesus? Can you start your own lunch-bag ministry, offer to volunteer with a local organization, or take meals to shut-ins? Ask the Lord to guide you.

The Rt. Rev. Gary Lillibridge

RESPOND

Day 31

QUALITIES OF A DISCIPLE / READ LUKE 17:1-10

In the passages just before this one, Jesus has been alternatively addressing the Pharisees and his disciples.

This see-saw pattern in Luke most likely indicates that, while Jesus was speaking directly to one group or the other, the second group was present and listening to what he was saying. Therefore, both groups heard everything Jesus said in chapters 15 and 16. One thing they both heard, in one form or another, was Jesus' message to avoid behaviors often practiced by the Pharisees.

As we begin chapter 17, Jesus now turns his attention back to the disciples. It is unclear whether the Pharisees are still present—they could be.

This passage (17:1-10) falls into four distinct sections. In verses 1-2, Jesus points out to his disciples that it is not possible for them (or us) to live in a world free of temptation. But, as bad as succumbing to temptation and sin is, Jesus' real wrath in these verses is directed to those who lead people into sin, those who create a stumbling block for others.

Verses 3-4 teach us the importance of forgiveness in the Christian life. The lesson begins with Jesus' exhortation to *"Pay attention to yourselves!"* (17:3). This is a good remember all the time, but especially when temptation comes knocking at your door—"pay attention!" Jesus then goes on to use the number seven to underscore the limitless nature of forgiveness. His teaching was quite a contrast to the rabbis' conventional wisdom that offering forgiveness to someone *three times* was the mark of a near perfect person. Jesus takes the rabbinic standard, doubles it, and then adds one for good measure—seven. But not seven times over a lifetime; seven times *in a day!* In other words, there is no limit to the number of times the Christian must forgive someone if true repentance is expressed. Jesus uses the number seven (and, in Matthew 18:22, *"seventy times seven"*) to represent this boundless forgiveness.

I'm sure we would all agree that this is good news for each and every one of us. As I am fond of saying, I don't want what I deserve; I want mercy. In the Lord's Prayer, we say "Forgive us our sins as we forgive those who sin against us." One way of understanding this phrase is to hear it this way: "God, please use the same standard of forgiveness on me that I am using on everyone else." Remember, then, to be careful what you pray for! Jesus is instructing us through these two short verses in Luke that the Christian standard of forgiveness must far exceed the best the world offers.

Jesus then reveals to his disciples that faith is the greatest force in the world (vs.5-6). He does this using vivid language (which was customary at the time) to assure us that even when something looks completely impossible, it can become possible when approached with faith. Think about it. If you approach a situation and say, "It can't be done," it likely will not be done. But if you say, "It must be done," then there is a very real possibility it will be done. The disciples were, and we are, like cracked jars of clay (2 Corinthians 4:7). When it comes to faith, we leak. We all need a refilling of our faith from time to time. "Give us this day, our daily bread (faith!)."

Lastly, and again using very vivid language, Jesus tells us in verses 7-10 that we can never put God in our debt. When we do our very best for Jesus, we simply are doing what is expected. God's bar is high and requires much; denying one's self is an integral part of the life of a faithful disciple. William Barclay, in his commentary on this passage, notes that the fourth verse of the hymn, "When I Survey the Wondrous Cross" nicely sums up what is expected:[21]

---

21. Barclay, *The Gospel of Luke*, p. 225.

Were the whole realm of nature mine,
That were an offering far too small;
Love so amazing, so divine,
Demands my soul, my life, my all.[22]

— Isaac Watts, 1707

REFLECT

In these ten verses, there are four sections regarding discipleship. Make a list of attitudes and qualities you hear described in these verses. Which ones come rather easily for you? Which ones are more difficult? Have you ever faced a challenge that demanded your all? Was it scary or exciting? The Christian life can be both; but the good news is, Jesus promises to be our constant companion every step along The Disciple's Way.

The Rt. Rev. Gary Lillibridge

RESPOND

_____

_____

_____

_____

_____

22. *Episcopal Hymnal 1982* (New York: Church Publishing Inc., 1982), Hymn 474.

Day 32

POWER AND PRESENCE / READ LUKE 17:11-19

How does the way we view Jesus shape the way we see ourselves and see the world around us?

Jesus and his disciples, while on their journey to Jerusalem, are about to enter a village, presumably located somewhere along the border between Israel and Samaria. The exact location is not revealed by Luke; however, it would have been uncommon for Jews to travel through Samaritan territory. It is noteworthy that one of the conflicts dividing the Jews and Samaritans was the location of the true temple, the one place on earth ordained by God for sacrifice and worship. For the Jews, it was the Temple in Jerusalem, while for the Samaritans it was on Mount Gerizim.

Knowing the history of antipathy between the Samaritans and the Jews, one would assume Jesus and the disciples are entering a Jewish village, not a Samaritan one. (Luke, being an artful storyteller, is, I believe, intentionally ambiguous about the location.) Jesus, still on the outskirts of the village, hears ten lepers who remain at a distance shout to him, *"Jesus, Master, have mercy on us"* (17:13). Luke says that when Jesus saw them and recognized their need, he immediately directed them to go and show themselves to a priest. As one, they turn and go, presumably to find a priest. Along the way, they are miraculously healed of their skin lesions. Luke tells us that *one* of the ten, on realizing he had been made well, turned back praising God with a loud voice.

It is what Luke reveals next that alters the significance of this miraculous healing relative to other New Testament healing accounts (e.g., Luke 5:12-

14). Luke reveals that the only leper to return and thank Jesus, falling at his feet, was a Samaritan. Jesus highlights the irony of the situation with his three questions: *"Were not ten cleansed? Where are the nine? Was no one found to return and give praise to God expect this foreigner?"* (17:17-18).

The Samaritan's actions indicate the he saw more than clear skin on his body; in falling at Jesus' feet in gratitude and praise, he recognized Jesus as someone who had authority, God's authority, and he signified his belief with an act of reverence. (The symbolism of a Samaritan worshiping at the feet of Jesus should not be overlooked. It shows that neither the Jerusalem Temple nor Mount Gerizim is the real focal point for worship—it is Jesus.) The Samaritan alone among the ten lepers recognized the power of God's kingdom breaking into the present in the person of Jesus.

It appears that while the nine Jewish lepers saw that they were healed, they did not perceive the power and presence of God in the person of Jesus. Their hearts were not full of awe and thanks for God's work in their lives. And yet all ten shared a religious and historical framework that should have given them such insight!

Each of us spends the early years of our life learning and crafting a narrative about who we are. This becomes our framework for understanding and interacting with the world. The same is true for our Christian life. What we come to believe about Jesus and who he truly is frames the way we see God and understand his (and our) mission in the world.

Let us ask God to give us the eyes to see Jesus as the Samaritan man did—to see the very power and presence of God working through him to heal and restore, even today, in our very midst.

REFLECT

You may not recall precisely when you first encountered the risen Christ. However, since then, how has your perception and understanding of Jesus changed? Has Jesus, through the work of the Holy Spirit, reshaped your narrative, your way of seeing and interacting with people and the world? May Luke's recounting of the healing of the ten lepers help us more deeply understand who Jesus truly is and our own journey with him.

The Rev. Greg Buffone

RESPOND

Day 33

FALSE EXPECTATIONS / READ LUKE 17:20-21

Even a cursory reading of the Gospels reveals the strained nature of the relationship between the Jewish leaders and Jesus.

The tension and animosity build during Jesus' public ministry, culminating in a murderous intent that leads to Jesus' death on a cross. What was it about this man that created such anger and a desire to end Jesus' life?

In Jesus' time, cultural and religious expectations anticipated a coming Messiah—a Warrior King—who would deliver Israel from its Roman oppressors. This Messiah would set himself up as ruler, and thereby inaugurate the kingdom of God on earth. With expectations like these, Israel and its religious leaders had definite ideas about what kind of empirical signs would accompany and identify the Messiah—a mental checklist if you will.

Not only did Jesus fall short of their expectations, he actually (in their minds) blasphemed by claiming to be one with God! Jesus dared to publicly flaunt the religious leaders' interpretation of Mosaic Law and repeatedly call out their hypocritical behavior. Suffice it to say that Jesus threatened the Jewish rulers' security and power. Yet, they had to tread cautiously because many were following him. Jesus' controversial public ministry even raised the fearful possibility that the Roman occupiers would intervene should his popularity among the people lead to open revolt—something the Jewish leaders wished to avoid at all costs. This seems a sufficient list of factors to make for a rocky relationship.

So, with this background in mind, let's consider today's brief passage from Luke 17. The Pharisees are pressing Jesus for an answer to the question:

When is the kingdom of God coming?

The Pharisees' question implies that they are still anticipating the coming of the kingdom as a future event and not a current reality. Not surprising, given their expectations. Jesus' answer is not unlike one given earlier in Luke 11:29-32: *"The kingdom of God is not coming in ways that can be observed…"* (17:20). In other words, the coming of the kingdom will not be characterized by the empirical signs you expect. *"For behold,"* he adds, *"the kingdom of God is among you"* (17:21b).

Jesus' declaration of the kingdom being present and active (while not eliminating a future manifestation when the Son of Man returns) is a clear rebuke of the Pharisees. It is a condemnation of their failure to see and experience the kingdom being exhibited in the person and works of Jesus.

There is an obvious parallel between the Pharisees and the nine lepers—neither group perceived God at work in the person of Jesus. The inability of the Pharisees to see and understand Jesus as the Messiah, the Anointed of God—despite hearing his teaching and witnessing his miracles—is, in a way, not so surprising. Their presuppositions and preconceived ideas about the Messiah were so firmly entrenched that they were blind to the presence and working of God in their midst.

When I consider the inability of the Jewish leaders and people of Jesus' day to see "God with them" in the person of Jesus, it gives me pause. How could a people who had been the recipients of God's revelation through the prophets; experienced his miraculous deliverance from Egypt; zealously observed the Law; and participated in Temple worship for centuries get it so wrong? If they could fail to perceive God working in and through Jesus, might we?

I suspect we're all equally vulnerable to having our ability to see Jesus clouded by our expectations and desires. As I look back over my own faith journey, I must admit it's been true for me. Because of this, I believe it's worthwhile to consider that, in order to see something or someone clearly and to deepen our understanding, it's often necessary to unlearn the things we thought we knew. This can be painful. But it opens the door to learning something new—something more real and more accurate.

If we are to be Jesus' disciples, it's important that we see him for who he truly is. What might it take for you and me to be open to the idea that we may have gotten some things wrong; to be willing to be led by the Holy Spirit into seeing things from a divine perspective? If we are willing to do this, we will experience an awakening to God's vantage point and to his concern for the vulnerable, the oppressed, and those in need of justice. Be ready!

REFLECT

What presuppositions or prejudices might be coloring your view of Jesus and his work in your life? In what way is Jesus challenging you to reconsider how you relate to him and to the people around you? I encourage you to pray for a new awakening and understanding of your calling as you continue your journey with Jesus along The Disciple's Way.

The Rev. Greg Buffone

RESPOND

Day 34

THE MAIN THING / READ LUKE 17:23-37

Jesus seems to keep everyone a bit off balance.

I can only imagine that following Jesus as his disciple must have been unsettling—exciting, awe inspiring, yet often confounding. Of his followers, some fell away (John 6:60-69), but others, including the twelve, remained with him right up until his arrest.

Though Jesus' teaching style often relied on parables or analogies, he was unabashedly direct in proclaiming his primary purpose: doing the will of the Father. His words, his actions, the signs and miracles—everything he did was to ensure that the Father's redemptive purpose and work was accomplished, regardless of the cost. Earlier in Luke Gospel we're told that, *"When the days drew near for him to be taken up, he set his face to go to Jerusalem"* (9:51). Jesus was absolutely single-minded in regard to his ultimate mission, even though that commitment would require his suffering and death.

But there were other facets of Jesus' mission prior to Calvary. One of these was recruiting, discipling, and empowering a small group who would continue the work Jesus inaugurated with his sacrifice on the Cross—the ongoing work of redemption and transformation that would continue until his return.

When we encounter Jesus' disciples in today's reading, they are most likely still trying to discern the meaning of what their master just told the Pharisees about the kingdom of God—that it is right *"in the midst"* of them (17:21). Now Jesus turns to his followers and shares an even more enigmatic pronouncement.

While Jesus anticipated what awaited him in Jerusalem, it is almost certain that, at this point, the disciples were envisioning a much more optimistic outcome. They were expecting the inauguration of God's earthly kingdom; never imagining, despite Jesus' warnings, the rejection and crucifixion of their Messiah.

Knowing the disciples' frame of mind, Jesus again tries in the first few verses of today's passage to correct their understanding by warning them that the kingdom is not imminent, at least not a kingdom in the form they anticipate—a seeming paradox considering that he's just told the Pharisees that the kingdom is among them. He now reveals to his disciples that there will be a time of waiting and anticipation between his suffering and his eventual return, a time when many will become complacent and distracted by commonplace activities of daily living. Then suddenly, unexpectedly, the end will come—just like the flood and the burning of Sodom stunned the people of Noah and Lot's days.

In that day, Jesus said, there will be no wondering *where* or *when* any longer, for his coming will be manifest with dramatic signs, in fact a cosmic revelation of his return and the initiation of the reign of God on earth.

Thinking over today's text brought to mind the movie *City Slickers*.[23] In that film, Jack Parlance, who plays the rough, crusty cowboy named Curly wants little to do with Mitch, played by Billy Crystal. Mitch has come out West in an attempt to deal with his midlife crisis. After a cattle stampede, Curly and Mitch set out together to track down stray cows, forcing them to spend time together. During this joint mission, Curly softens his feelings toward Mitch. Sensing that Mitch is a bit lost, Curly tells him that his life will take on meaning when he discovers the *one thing* that is most important to him.

---

23. *City Slickers*. Directed by Ron Underwood. 1991. New York: Castle Rock Entertainment.

I believe in this passage Jesus is warning his followers that there will be many things to distract our attention and divert our energies from the main thing: *faithfully following Jesus and continuing the redemptive work of God in the world.* While our day-to-day responsibilities of living cannot, and should not, be ignored, Jesus warns us not to make the necessities of this world the main thing. The things of this world find their true meaning and value in relation to him. Only in Jesus will we find meaning and fulfillment in this life and in the age to come.

REFLECT

Jesus wants us to make the main thing the main thing every day of our lives. What activities or concerns keep you in a state of distraction from the main thing? What would it take for you to minimize these distractions? Take a moment to pray and ask the Savior to help you relinquish to him your concerns, so that you can return your focus to following him and being about his work in the world.

The Rev. Greg Buffone

RESPOND

_____

_____

_____

_____

Day 35

WILL HE FIND FAITH? / READ LUKE 18:1-8

Do you ever find yourself longing for Jesus to return, to come quickly and establish his reign on the earth?

I must admit that there are some days when I look around at the violence, the injustice, the suffering all around us, and the seemingly chaotic nature of life, and I want Jesus to return that very day and put things right. That sense of helplessness and despair for the state of the world may be the feeling Jesus is addressing in Luke 18:1 when he tells us we are *"always to pray and not lose heart."*

Jesus has been addressing the expectations and speculation of both the Pharisees and his disciples regarding the coming kingdom. Essentially, his message to them is not to be distracted by the "when" or the "where" of the full coming of the kingdom of God. At the right time, God will act. But what are they and we, his disciples, to do in the meantime? Are we simply to wait and pray?

The Parable of the Unjust Judge has something to say in answer to these questions. Consider the archetypal roles Jesus sets in opposition within the parable: the judge and the widow. These roles are sharply contrasted in Palestinian Jewish society of the day. The role of judge was well established from the time of Moses and held standing and authority within the culture. Jesus describes the judge as someone who respects and fears neither God nor man—a characterization that clearly labels this judge as manifestly unsuited to the role and unlikely to render justice for justice's sake (2 Chronicles 19:4-7).

The role of the widow epitomizes those who are powerless in the Jewish culture. As a woman, with no rights of inheritance, a widow would be left with few resources and no social standing after the death of her husband. Widows, particularly those without sons, were completely dependent on the compassion and largess of the community for support and for any access to the social, religious, or judicial systems.

So, who prevails in this parable—the powerful judge or the helpless widow? The judge does not truly desire to see justice done, but because of the widow's persistence in seeking a just adjudication of her grievance, the judge is beaten into submission. The widow prevails! Jesus underscores this surprising story with two questions: Will not God give justice to his elect? And, will the Son of Man find faith on the earth upon his return?

The first question highlights the stark contrast between the unconcern of the unjust judge and the beneficent character of God. If an unrighteous judge can be compelled to meet out justice, how much more will a loving God respond to the appeals of his beloved children? This assurance should be a strong encouragement to the disciples and to us, to put our trust in God's mercy and justice. The answer is "Yes, God will give justice to his elect."

We might assume Jesus tells this parable to the disciples simply to encourage them to persistently seek God's goodness in the face of persecution and adversity, and not to be discouraged when they must endure for a time. But that would discount the significance of the roles, the widow and the judge, through which Jesus chose to make his point.

Throughout Holy Scripture, God's concern for orphans, widows, the poor, the stranger, and the vulnerable is evident. This is true not only in the Law of Moses in the Old Testament, but in Jesus' station in life, his birth, his profession, the people he openly accepted and spent time with, and his teaching. Consider just two examples of Jesus' teaching on the importance of caring for the vulnerable: Luke 14:12-13 and Matthew 25:31-46. In both texts, Jesus makes it clear that the oppressed are important to God and that he expects that we, the elect, will address their material needs as well as ensure they have access to the social, religious, and judicial systems of our society.

Now let's turn to the second question: Will the Son of Man find faith on the earth when he returns? This question seems to be rhetorical—a challenge even. What exactly does Jesus mean by it?

Faith, in a New Testament context, is never simply about believing facts or embracing creedal statements. While faith is never less than belief, it is always more than that. It is about trusting God as we know him in Jesus the Christ to such an extent that our faith informs *who we are* and *how we live* in response to God's grace and love. Faith is what draws us into the heart of God and moves us to love what and who he loves.

James reminds us that a living faith is manifest not just in belief, but in action (James 2:14-17). It is the demonstration of love for one another, including those outside the community of faith, that identifies us as disciples of Jesus before the watching world (John 13:35). Will Jesus find such faith in us?

REFLECT

Faith, living faith, is always manifest in action, in service, in sacrifice, in persistence, and sometimes in suffering. Think of strong examples of living faith around you. How do these examples inspire you? How is your faith in Jesus transforming the way you see and relate to the people you encounter?

The Rev. Greg Buffone

RESPOND

_____

_____

_____

_____

Week Six

SELFLESS HUMILITY

And will not God give justice to his elect, who cry to him day and night? Will he delay long over them? I tell you; he will give justice to them speedily. Nevertheless, when the Son of Man comes, will he find faith on earth?

LUKE 18:7-8

CONSIDER

Do you find your value in comparison to others or in humble embrace of God's mercy?

Day 36

THE COMPARISON GAME / READ LUKE 18:9-14

When I was at the university, we had several large classes with hundreds of people in them, some close to a thousand.

These were called "weed out" classes. The key to not getting weeded out was to make sure you were in the top tier of the class. I learned very quickly that the tests were graded on a curve—even if you got 50% of the questions wrong, you could still make an "A" as long as you got more answers right than 90% of the other students. In these classes, rather than being judged by an objective standard, you were judged in comparison to others. Personally, I grew to resent grading on the curve because it wasn't based on merit, it was based on comparison to your peers.

Many people live as if life is graded on a curve. They play the comparison game. Success and failure are measured in horizontal relationship to others. "So long as I'm doing better than the other guy, I'm okay." Comparisons may use all types of measures: financial, rank, privilege, access, accomplishment, pedigree, beauty, strength. We all have our measures. The world's values set us against one another and urge us to compete and compare.

How many of us have done exactly what the Pharisee in today's story did? We've looked at another human being and thought to ourselves, "I thank God I'm not like that guy! I'm living my life well compared to his messy one." In our heads, we may even have a mental scorecard and check off some of our winning qualities: generous, honest (most of the time), successful in business, raising well-behaved (reasonably, anyway) children, etc. We conclude we are the "good guys," decent people all around.

The Pharisee's aim in Jesus' story was to justify himself in his own sight and in the sight of God. His prayer was essentially a list of his good qualities! He didn't ask God for mercy because he didn't think he needed any, especially in comparison to that tax collector standing over there.

How often do we make ourselves righteous by discounting others or another "one" in particular? Such an attitude requires that we hold someone else in contempt. I've noticed that religious people who speak self-righteously often have a certain critical spirit that creeps in. Maybe you've noticed this in yourself. Or maybe you've been on the receiving end of it. It can happen in worship when we start to focus on the people around us instead of the Lord: "Why does she always raise her hands so high? It's not considerate to those behind her." Or, "That guy is always looking at his phone during the sermon. Must not be very spiritual." Perhaps he is following along the Scripture passage online! A critical spirit is a symptom of pride.

Now let's look at the tax collector. He doesn't measure himself against the righteousness of others in the room. Instead, he measures himself against the holiness of God. He understands that, according to God's standards, getting 50% correct never counts as a passing grade. The only way he'll ever be accepted in God's sight is if he receives mercy. No self-congratulations for doing better than the other guy. His prayer proves he knows the truth, *"God, be merciful to me, a sinner!"* (18:13).

As the Psalmist writes,

> The LORD looks down from heaven on the children of man,
> > to see if there are any who understand,
> > who seek after God.
> They have all turned aside; together they have become corrupt;

> there is none who does good,
>
> not even one.
>
> — Psalm 14:2-3

And in another place, he writes,

> If you, O LORD, should mark iniquities
>
> O Lord, who could stand?
>
> But with you there is forgiveness,
>
> that you may be feared.
>
> — Psalm 130:3-4

This sinful tax collector who knows who he is before God also seems to understand the character of God. He knows the Lord is merciful. So even though he recognizes his unworthiness to come into the Lord's sanctuary, he cries out in his approach—*"God, be merciful to me, a sinner!"* (18:13). He is aware of and relying on God's mercy and grace.

Thank God that justification comes only from the Lord and not from how we compare to others. Thank God that he's not counting our sins against us. His mercies are everlasting!

I want to caution you about something. When we read this story, we need to avoid the danger of comparing ourselves to the Pharisee, thinking, "Thank God I'm not like that self-righteous, legalistic Pharisee! At least I know I'm a sinner." We would be doing just as the Pharisee did with the tax collector—making a horizontal comparison in which we try to justify ourselves in relationship to someone else.

The tax collector saw the depth of his depravity and the magnitude of God's grace. He focused not on horizontal comparisons, but on his vertical relationship with the Lord. Let us do the same.

REFLECT

Do you play the comparison game—do you find yourself feeling good about yourself in contrast to others, or condemning yourself? Perhaps some of both? In one instance, we are feeling morally superior to others and, in the other, we are refusing to accept God's mercy. Neither are the marks of a disciple. Why not pray now, along with the tax collector: *"God, be merciful to me, a sinner!"*

The Rev. Charlie Holt

RESPOND

_____

_____

_____

_____

Day 37

RECEIVING CHILDREN, RECEIVING THE KINGDOM
/ READ LUKE 18:15-17

One of my favorite parts of my job is giving the children's sermon during the worship service.

I am often amazed at the pure, unbridled zeal that children have toward the Lord. They sing, dance, make hand motions, and engage the sermon eagerly. Children are instinctively drawn to Jesus; they seem to perceive in him the humility and innocence they experience in themselves.

Unfortunately, as adults, we are often mildly embarrassed when the kids become "overly exuberant" in church. We dismiss them as being too young and idealistic to understand; we put their zeal in the category of fun and play. We believe, as adults, that we need to focus on "more important things." Perhaps this is why the disciples in today's story shoo the children away. They're just kids, running and playing. They aren't to be taken seriously.

Once I was in the midst of a sermon to a full congregation when a tiny voice cried out "yeah!" at just the right moment. It couldn't have been timed better. Everyone in the church laughed in delight. I wondered, "Why doesn't the whole congregation respond with such joy at the Word of the Lord and the telling of his awesome work?" We could use a little more enthusiasm in the expression of our passion during worship—childlike enthusiasm.

We adults call our reserve "maturity," but sometimes I think it's just a mask for hardheartedness and cynicism. As we go through life, our hearts get battered and even break under the weight of the abuses and disappointments we experience. We lose our humble innocence. Yet the Lord says that if we do not receive the kingdom of God like a child, we shall not enter it.

So how does a child receive the kingdom?

Every young man is born with the heart of a prince destined for great things— to slay monsters and conquer kingdoms. Every young woman is born with the heart of a princess—to love life, beauty, and romance. Fairytales and myths express this childlike imagination that longs for the beautiful, the noble, and the true. God has indeed set eternity in the hearts of all, especially children.

Children receive the kingdom of God with their whole hearts and with their whole imaginations, with a humble innocence, uninhibited.

But sadly, young imaginative hearts can gradually become hard hearts. It takes time, but the faith of a child is often lost as we age. Sadly, I see it happening earlier and earlier—young hearts growing cold to God and calling it "cool."

The gift of the humble innocence of a child, then, shows the way back to God for all of us. We all long for the attributes of God—his beauty, nobility, and strength. We long for God himself. We were made for abundant relationship with him. Yet as we grow, we sometimes inhibit childlike faith not only in the children, but in ourselves. We learn through our experience with evil, suffering, and betrayal not to lead with our hearts, but to self-protect and guard them.

Jesus would have us recover our abundant life in him! Our idealistic dreams and awe-inspired sense of wonder and amazement must return. Watch the children in worship and their exuberant zeal and delight in the things of

God—you will see the path back. They teach us to relate to his kingdom with humble innocence. Soft hearts desire the Lord.

REFLECT

Have you recently attended a children's service? What did you observe in watching the children? What about the adults? Do you find yourself growing anxious at the zeal of children or could you enter into that childlike faith yourself? Ask the Lord to give you back a childlike enthusiasm for him.

The Rev. Charlie Holt

RESPOND

_____
_____
_____
_____

Day 38

THE PROBLEM OF WEALTH AND POWER / READ LUKE 18:18-30

In today's reading, Jesus says, *"How difficult it is for those who have wealth to enter the kingdom of God! For it is easier for a camel to go through the eye of a needle than for a rich person to enter the kingdom of God"* (18:24-25).

What does Jesus mean by the "eye of a needle?"

There is an interpretation of today's passage that defines the eye of a needle as a skinny gate in Jerusalem that a camel can fit through if it is unburdened of its bundles and then repacked—but the camel can still get through. This reading of the passage completely misses the point. What Jesus is saying is that threading the eye of an actual needle with a real camel is impossible!

What the parable is teaching is: Beware the sin of self-sufficiency. When you have everything you need, do you really need God?

Let's look at Jesus' encounter with the rich ruler that leads up to the "eye of the needle" comment.

When the rich man asks Jesus, *"Good teacher, what must I do to inherit eternal life?"* (18:18), Jesus quotes him a partial list of the Ten Commandments: *"Do not commit adultery, Do not murder, Do not steal, Do not bear false witness, Honor your father and mother."* The man replies, *"All these I have kept from my youth."* The wealthy ruler had lived a good life. From a human standpoint, he was what we call a "good guy." He is the kind of person you would like your daughter to marry—an upstanding person, with money! But notice Jesus had quoted only five of the Ten Commandments, the back half. The first five have to do with a heart that is dedicated to loving God above all else. Remember there are two great commandments, which sum up the ten; the first and greatest is to love the Lord your God with all your heart, mind, soul, and strength.

When Jesus then challenged his questioner to sell everything he had and follow him, the rich man came up short—very short. He went away sad for he was extremely wealthy. I do not think that Jesus' word to the rich ruler is for everyone. Not everyone is called to sell everything. But the passage does serve to show that wealth can have a powerful hold on our lives. It can be an idol. If you were given a direct challenge from the Lord to dispossess everything, could you do it?

When I was in college, I did a thought exercise—of all the things I owned, what would I have the hardest time giving up? At that time, I could fit all my worldly possessions into my 1978 Oldsmobile Delta 88. While it was a big car, it wasn't much. As I inventoried my stuff, I realized I could give away almost everything for Jesus, including the car. But there was *one thing* I really loved, my 50-gallon fish tank. Funny, looking back, that was the one item I brought into my marriage that my wife despised! When we went off to seminary, it was the one item that couldn't make the trip. So, I actually did have to give up that prized possession for the Lord. He has a sense of humor. And giving that tank away made my wife happy too.

In contrast to college days, it now takes a semitruck to move my family and all of our stuff. But we strive to hold it all loosely. As I have grown in my dependence on the Lord, I have learned that there isn't any material thing in my life that I would not willingly give up for him. I have signed a quit claim deed to God—it all belongs to him.

When we have wealth, it's easy to deceive ourselves into thinking we've got it all together. We can handle whatever arises. We feel secure. Interestingly,

Jesus had more to say about money than any other topic he discussed. Money, he said, is the chief rival to God for our devotion.

Why is it so hard for the rich to get into heaven? Honestly, because the rich seemingly don't need God. Money can buy a lot of things and solve a lot of problems. But it's a lie that the wealthy don't need God. Every human being has the same need for God. The apostle Peter rightly observes in today's story that if a good guy like the rich ruler can't get into heaven, then it's impossible for anyone. That is the point.

Getting into heaven on our own power is impossible. There is no amount of self-help, will power, or wealth that can earn (or buy) our way into eternal life. It is a gift! An act of loving grace on God's part is required for *any* person to get into heaven: *"What is impossible with man is possible with God"* (18:27).

The difference between the rich and the poor is that self-sufficiency does not mask the need for God's grace for those who have little. The poor have nothing to rely on but God. That is why we are *all* called to be "poor in spirit"—to realize that we need God to rescue our souls from sin and to give us eternal life.

REFLECT

If Jesus were to challenge you to dispossess yourself of all your wealth and belongings, what would be the hardest thing to give away—what would be your "fish tank?" How much do you really need God's provision in your life? Ask God to show you your genuine need for him this week.

The Rev. Charlie Holt

RESPOND

_____

_____

_____

_____

Day 39

INEVITABLE SUFFERING / READ LUKE 18:31-34

The Cross of Jesus can be hard to understand.

Why would God send such an amazing gift as his Son, who teaches with authority, leads with compassion, and has the power to drive out the legions of hell, only to see him dishonored and executed with a cruel, torturous death?

The prophet Isaiah anticipates the world's profound confusion over the vocation of the Messiah: *"Who has believed what he has heard from us? And to whom has the arm of the LORD been revealed?"* (Isaiah 53:1). No matter how many times Jesus explained to his disciples that he would have to die, they just couldn't grasp it.

After the Crucifixion and Resurrection, Jesus' disciples would gradually understand. They would make the meaning of the Cross the central point of their gospel message. The Messiah came to give his life in exchange for the lives of his people. In the words of the prophet Isaiah, *"Surely he has borne our infirmities and carried our diseases…he was wounded for our transgressions, crushed for our iniquities; upon him was the punishment that made us whole, and by his bruises we are healed…The Lord has laid on him the iniquity of us all"* (Isaiah 53:4-6, NRSV).

The Cross is the most important element of the Christian gospel. By his wounds, we are healed. The punishment that we deserved was upon him.

The prophets of old had spelled out the importance and significance of the coming Messiah's death. Yet even to this day it remains an enigma to so many in the world. How could the death of one man on a Roman cross 2,000 years ago have any bearing on my life? People die all the time. The Romans killed tens of thousands. So what?

For the disciples, contemplating such a fate as early death for their beloved rabbi was unfathomable for personal reasons. They loved Jesus. They were also pinning their hopes and dreams for a better life on him and his coming kingdom. Somehow, Jesus' teaching about the Cross did not compute.

In our day, the message of the Cross often falls on deaf ears for another reason: the seeming foolishness or irrelevance of its message. People are quite content with self-reliance and their own success. They do not see a need for salvation, grace, or eternal life. For the secular minded person, Jesus has some encouraging principles to live by, but his hardcore call to give it all up for him—well, that is a walk too far. The modern individual says, "Everything in moderation. I have a beautiful, wrinkle-free life. Morals and values, yes. But martyrdom for God—that seems a bit extreme."

But the way of a true disciple leads to a cross. There is no getting around it. Jesus said, if you want to be my disciple, you must pick up your cross, die daily, and follow me. Your commitment to Jesus' way will be tested. The opposition of this sinful world will either prove or disprove your commitment to him.

There was a man in my congregation who was falsely accused by the Department of Justice, framed by members of his own company, and used as a scapegoat to protect those who had broken the law. Ironically, this man was a person of absolute integrity. He also had deep faith in Christ. I watched him bear up under the pain of trial as his family stood by and prayed. He refused to "go along to get along," and ended up paying a worldly price. Yet, through every moment, I witnessed his resolve to follow Jesus grow stronger. He became more and more of an evangelist, to the point of leading Bible studies in a maximum security prison. This man picked up his cross and followed Jesus.

We live in a sinful and broken world. The disciple of Jesus will suffer—it is inevitable. The pain may even come from those closest to us. Yet we follow a crucified Lord. His way is foolishness to a world that values celebrity over integrity, success over faithfulness, and power over people. But God has chosen the foolish things of this world to shame the wise (1 Corinthians 1:27).

The Cross of Jesus is the wisdom and power of God for the salvation of the world. Will you proclaim it? Will you pick up your cross to follow him?

REFLECT

Are there aspects of Jesus' Crucifixion that you still do not understand? Ask God to help you. How have you borne your own cross? Have others misunderstood your decisions to sacrifice for the sake of following Jesus? If so, you are in good company. Keep following Jesus on The Disciple's Way!

The Rev. Charlie Holt

RESPOND

_____

_____

_____

_____

Day 40

TOTAL TRANSFORMATION / READ LUKE 18:35-43

When the Son of Man comes, will he find faith on the earth?

This question posed by Jesus in the opening passage of Luke 18 is a powerful one. It admits the possibility that Jesus won't find faith when he returns—at least not the kind he is looking for.

What kind of faith does the Son of Man want to find on his second coming? Throughout this chapter, Luke presents stories that reveal the answer.

The first story is that of a repentant tax collector who cries out, *"God, be merciful to me, a sinner"* (18:13). Humility, Jesus explains, leads to kingdom exaltation (18:14). The second example is that of a child. The disciples seek to prevent children from coming to Jesus, but he lifts them up as examples of the type of faith we need to enter the kingdom of God—one has to *"receive the kingdom of God like a child…"* (18:17).

In the next story, the question, *"What must I do to inherit eternal life?"* is asked by a rich ruler. Jesus instructs the man to renounce his idolatry of riches: *"One thing you still lack. Sell all that you have and distribute to the poor, and you will have treasure in heaven; and come, follow me"* (18:22).

After the man walks away sullen, the disciples remark to Jesus on the seeming impossibility for anyone to enter the kingdom of God with such a high threshold of total self-sacrifice. Jesus agrees: *"What is impossible with man is possible with God"* (18:27). The man's question was based on a false premise. He asked, *"…what must I do to inherit eternal life?"* Notice the word "do." Salvation is not a payment God owes us for faithfulness to the Law (which we could never keep perfectly); it is a gracious gift. As Paul taught the Ephesians, *"For by grace you have been saved through faith. And this is not your own doing; it is the gift of God, not a result of works, so that no one may boast"* (Ephesians 2:8-9). The rich ruler lacked the *faith* to believe that Jesus could provide for him, sustain him, and ultimately save him, rather than his riches.

Now we come to today's passage. Jesus encounters a blind beggar. The beggar calls out, *"Jesus, Son of David, have mercy on me!"* (18:38). When Jesus hears him, he commands the beggar to be brought to him and asks, *"What do you want me to do for you?"* (18:41). The blind man replies, *"Lord, let me recover my sight"* (18:41). Notice, though this man is poor, he does not ask for material provision; he asks instead to be healed.

Consider the implications of the blind beggar's request for healing. If it were to be granted by Jesus, the man would have to learn a whole new way of being in and relating to the world. He would have to find employment other than begging. Being made well would significantly change all the relationships in his life, which were built around his blindness and dependency. He would have to be responsible in a whole new way. Yet, despite all the required changes, the blind man asks for full healing, nonetheless.

How many of us come to Jesus looking for a solution to just a symptom of our real problem? We don't want to deal with the deeper issue. The blind man does not ask Jesus to alleviate a symptom (material poverty), but to address his real problem, a lack of sight. He seeks total healing, *"Lord, let me recover my sight."*

The blind man had it right. We all need to be crying out to Jesus to have mercy on us. We will not be saved by what we do for God, but by what he does for us. We need to ask Jesus not just to alleviate the temporary problems we have, but to heal us completely.

I've observed that when a person truly receives the Lord's healing in their life, the systems they've constructed around themselves and their brokenness must also change. This kind of radical transformation is difficult. It takes courage. Yet this is the type of faith the Son of Man is looking for—a faith that desires wholeness and healing to the core of our being. For Jesus responds to the man, *"Receive your sight; your faith has made you well"* (18:42).

As we move toward the close of Luke's travel narrative, the Gospel writer's encouragement to us, his readers, is to demonstrate the kind of faith the Son of Man desires to find when he returns—unwavering faith that is willing to endure hardship along the way, committing everything to Jesus, and asking for complete life transformation.

Is this the kind of faith you have?

REFLECT

Is your "faith" like that of the rich ruler—are you happy to believe but unwilling to give up whatever it takes to follow Jesus? Or, are you more like the trusting child or the blind beggar, willing to trust Jesus completely to have mercy on you, heal you, and bring you to eternal life? Ask Jesus now for the kind of faith he is looking for…and be ready for a total life transformation.

The Rev. Charlie Holt

RESPOND

_____

_____

_____

_____

Day 41

HELPING OTHERS SEE JESUS / READ LUKE 19:1-10

Jesus came to seek and to save that which was lost.

Zacchaeus was a short little fellow, not just short in stature but short in the estimation of his neighbors. He was a tax collector—a person considered to be a lowlife, willing to exploit his own people to profit from the enemy Romans. He was deemed unworthy of the kingdom of God because he was a "sinner."

Let's contrast Zacchaeus with the rich man from earlier in the chapter. We have a rich young ruler and a rich, short tax collector. They are both wealthy. They are both in high positions (one respected and one despised). They both encounter Jesus. Yet only one gains salvation while the other misses it.

Notice that, in his own estimation, the rich young ruler is high in status: "I have done everything that is expected of me to be a good person," he basically boasts. He judges himself worthy of salvation. But Jesus says the way to salvation for him is to sell all he has, give to the poor, and follow Jesus. The man becomes sad because he has great wealth. The story implies that he goes away, unwilling to obey Jesus, and thereby misses salvation.

Zacchaeus, on the other hand, received the negative judgment of others. He was considered unsavable. Yet, he does exactly what Jesus asked of the rich ruler. On his own initiative and as an act of repentance, he pledges to sell half his possessions to give to the poor and pay back four-fold any person he's cheated. Jesus asserts at the end of the story, *"Today salvation has come to this house"* (19:9).

Those who observed Jesus' encounter with the rich man asked, *"Then who can be saved?"* (18:26). The answer: A guy like Zacchaeus. Zacchaeus is what we would call a true "see"-ker. He wants to see Jesus because he longs to know who Jesus is. He was not content to let Jesus pass through town without catching a glimpse. He was even willing to overcome the obstacle (and possibly ridicule) of the crowd to climb a tree to lock eyes with the Savior.

Today we have people who desperately need to get to know the Lord. Their lives are a wreck. They are broken. They may be going through a divorce, have lost a child or spouse, or hit economically hard times. Perhaps they've royally flubbed up in some aspect of life by committing an egregious sin they feel deeply guilty about.

Often these hurting souls come to church looking for something. What are they looking for? They're looking for the Savior! They know their need, though they may not be able to verbalize it. They know something inside of them is lacking. They are hopeful that when they walk into the midst of the body of Christ, they will find the presence of Jesus and he will find them—they will somehow discover the life and salvation they're seeking.

But now we come against the problem of the crowd—in this case, we the people of God. We are often in the way of the seeker, preventing him or her from seeing Jesus. We aren't looking out for people like Zacchaeus, and we certainly aren't making it easy for people like him to find Jesus. We're not seeing with the eyes of Jesus the lost person who enters our midst.

The times I feel most proud of our congregation is when I hear stories of how a person came in broken, needy, and hurting, and our congregation rallied around them, showing them the love of Jesus and the acceptance and welcome of God. We have many stories like this. In fact, they're a defining mark of our church. Does your congregation demonstrate the love of Jesus by your welcome to newcomers? *Zacchaeus, come right on in, let us show you Jesus.*

Zacchaeus, sadly, had to fight his way through the crowd to see Jesus, and what a shame. Sometimes we, too, miss the opportunity to help someone see Jesus. For a brief moment, perhaps, a seeker is giving the Lord a chance in this place, in our church, and we don't acknowledge them. We don't bother to say hi or smile at them. They walk in and they walk out, never to return. I've seen that happen, too. I've seen the story of Zacchaeus played out in church.

But Zacchaeus is exactly the type of person that Luke knows will be receptive to the gospel—just as we can often recognize those in need of Jesus. Luke's first readers may have related to Zacchaeus or known people like him who were ripe for the message of the kingdom. You may know some, too. Resolve not to let them miss seeing Jesus because of you. Instead, hold them up and help them see.

REFLECT

More than anything else, people need to be welcomed into the presence of Jesus to abide with him. Are you, like Zacchaeus, seeking not just to see the Lord, but to repent and obey him? To abide with him in a personal relationship? Are you ever blind to people who cross your path who desperately want to see Jesus? Ask God to open your eyes to them so you can help them see the Savior.

The Rev. Charlie Holt

RESPOND

_____

_____

_____

Day 42

ABOUT THE KING'S BUSINESS / READ LUKE 19:11-27

Luke closes his travel narrative with a vision for the stewardship of our very lives.

The Gospel writer tells us the occasion for this parable: *"…because [Jesus] was near to Jerusalem, and because they supposed the kingdom of God was to appear immediately"* (19:11). The parable Jesus tells is about the delegation of responsibility to "servants" by a nobleman while he is away in a far country, receiving for himself "a kingdom."

While the nobleman is gone, there is a rejection of him by the larger citizenry. In the context of the travel narrative, this could only point to the rejection of another king, Jesus, by the corrupt leadership and other unbelieving members of the population. The servants represent Jesus' trusted disciples. The emphasis of the story is not so much on the judgment of the citizens who reject the king, but on the judgment of the one servant who does nothing with the mina he's been given.

To bring the narrative back to the missionary call of the "seventy two" in the beginning of Luke's narrative, the entire point of this section comes down to a single question: Are you willing to follow Jesus and be used by him to "seek and save the lost" in the midst of a rebellious world?

Yes, there will be citizens who reject the nobleman's kingship, and they ultimately will be judged for their rejection of the king. But the main message here is directed toward the disciple "on the way," who is insecure in their faith. Will you be bold and take the risk of investing your "mina?" Or will you bury it in a handkerchief (19:20)? Those who are faithful with "a very little" will be given authority over much (19:17). *"I tell you that to everyone who has, more will be given, but from the one who has not, even what he has will be taken away"* (19:26).

You may not have thought much about this parable. Typically during stewardship time, we hear sermons on the Parable of the Talents (see Matthew 25:14-30), but Luke's Parable of the Mina is often overlooked by preachers. Though there are similarities, there are some very big differences between the two parables. Let's highlight one.

In Matthew's Parable of the Talents, the servants are given different amounts of money to steward, but all earn the same percentage of interest—a doubling of their initial investment. (The one who is given five talents earns five more; the one who receives two talents gains two more.) The only one who differs is the servant who received just one talent. He merely buries it, earning nothing. In this parable, the emphasis is on the diversity and variety of gifts—different levels of talent, experience, and resources. Though we've been given different talents, we are all called to exercise them faithfully to grow the kingdom of God.

In Luke's Parable of the Mina, in contrast, each of the ten servants get the *same* amount—one mina—but they reap different amounts of profit, with one servant earning nothing. Jesus is emphasizing something slightly different here. We have all been given the same "one mina" to invest—one life. With our life, we are all called to steward the message of salvation, though we will have varying results.

Let's look at the varying results of the servants in the story. The first took the king's one mina and made ten more. He is congratulated and put in charge of ten cities. The next earned five minas with the original one. He is given charge over five cities. There's something to be said here. Though these two servants earned varying amounts with the same investment, they were both rewarded! We have each been given one life to invest in the kingdom. We can do different things with that life. Some will multiply more for the kingdom and some will multiply less, but what the Lord is looking for is multiplication.

Now, the third person did nothing with his mina. He says, *"Lord, here is your mina, which I kept laid away in a handkerchief..."* He explains his thinking on why he did nothing with the mina: *"...for I was afraid of you, because you are a severe man. You take what you did not deposit, and reap what you did not sow"* (19:20-21). The third fellow's mentality is that the king takes for himself the fruit of other people's labor, and that is not fair. His problematic attitude is seen in our American culture. We have an ownership society. We own our property, our cars, our businesses. Since we have earned these things, we think they all belong to us. We don't see ourselves as those who have worked with material that was *given to us*—our bodies, minds, and the natural world. Nor do we acknowledge that all of this was given *by God*.

A better attitude is to see that we are the king's people going about the king's work with the king's money for the king's benefit. This is The Disciple's Way.

Two of the three servants in Luke's story have this attitude and they are rewarded by the king.

Has not Jesus purchased the disciple's life by giving his own? Jesus' death is now to be multiplied for the harvest of the world. The harvest is plentiful, but the workers are few. Jesus sowed his life and he reaps through us by giving us a season to reap and multiply the kingdom unto him—to invest the mina we've been given. When he comes back, he's going to be interested in this one question: What have we done with what we've been given?

REFLECT

We've all been given the same command—to invest our "mina" to multiply souls for the kingdom of God. Do you see your life as a gift from God, worthy of investing in his kingdom? Consider what it would look like for you to give all for King Jesus. You can follow him boldly on The Disciple's Way or you can self-protect. What will you do with your mina?

The Rev. Charlie Holt

RESPOND

_____

_____

_____

_____

The Study Guide

HOW TO GET THE MOST OUT OF THIS STUDY

As with any individual or small-group study of God's Word, you largely reap what you sow—or, as it is commonly put, you get out of it what you put into it. But additionally, there are guidelines that can help you get the most from the efforts you put in. Outlined below are some suggestions for you and your group to review before you get started.

1. Review the Table of Contents.

2. If you're hosting or facilitating a group, read the section entitled "Small Group Leader Helps." It lays out best practices for how to host or facilitate a healthy small group and avoid common mistakes. It's a great idea to review this material before your first meeting.

3. Adapt this book to the needs of your group. If a line of discussion leads to green pastures outside the scope of the book, enjoy the leading of the Good Shepherd. Feel free to ask, or allow other members to ask, insightful questions as the Holy Spirit leads.

4. Relax and remember you do not have to ask every question in your group discussion. There is a lot of material here. Feel free to skip questions as needed and linger over the ones where there is authentic conversation.

5. Enjoy the experience. Christian community should be characterized by joy and love. Encourage yourself and your group members to bear such fruit.

6. Pray before each session. Ask God to minister to you, the host, the facilitator, and every group member by name. Pray for the discussion, the fellowship, and the personal application.

7. Read the "Outline of Sessions" section on the following pages so you understand the flow of the session and how the study works.

Outline of Sessions

QUESTION

This opening question sets the tone for the week's study. Read it aloud in your group and encourage members to consider the answer as you move through the study.

KEY VERSE

Each session begins with a key verse. This verse is central to understanding the entire week's theme. You may want to memorize the key verses. By committing portions of God's Word to long-term memory, you will have them to refer to even when you don't have a Bible with you.

SESSION INTRODUCTION

This section briefly introduces the subject of the week's teaching video. The subject will also reflect the theme your group has been learning about in the week's daily devotions. You may wish to have a group member read this section aloud to the group.

OPENING PRAYER

A prayer from the Book of Common Prayer is included in each session that has been specially chosen to reflect the session's theme. You may read this aloud to begin the teaching time or have someone in your group lead in an opening prayer.

GETTING STARTED

We've included two "warm-up" questions to get your group talking some before you begin the video teaching. The questions often will help set up the teaching you're about to hear.

WATCH THE VIDEO

Play the video for your group, making sure the volume is adequate for all to hear and every member can see the video from where they're sitting.

STUDY NOTES

These pages provide a space to take notes as you watch the video or hear inspirational thoughts from the Lord or members of your group.

VIDEO NOTES

This section summarizes key points made in the video. It is useful if a lot of material has been covered in the teaching and you want to help "sum it up" for your group. Again, feel free to bypass this section if you feel it's not needed. Sometimes a thought question is included.

HEAR GOD'S WORD

Your group will read aloud a passage of Scripture related to the prior video teaching. A note why this section is so important: Throughout the travel narrative of Luke, crowds gathered around Jesus to hear his teaching. Jesus said "those who hear the word of God and keep it" are blessed. The command in Deuteronomy 6:4-9 which begins, "Hear, O Israel," was a familiar charge to any Jewish ears. In the Hebrew language, the word *shema* (used for "to hear" or "to listen") is actually the same word used for "to obey." Unlike in English, there is no such thing as passively listening in Hebrew. Luke is continually calling us to hear the words of Jesus. Our first task in this study, then, is to pay attention to the words of Jesus.

TAKE THESE WORDS TO HEART

This section includes questions about the Scripture passage you've just read. If our first step is to hear the Word of the Lord, our next step is to do something with it. True hearing requires faithful action. Hearing and doing are the key ingredients of faith. In community, we can wrestle with the meaning behind the parables and various teachings Jesus shares and determine how to apply them to our lives. As you study Luke, your group will consider overarching themes such as the idea of divine reversal—new and radical ways to understand our allegiances, our priorities, and our views of privilege and power. What better way to gain the fullest picture of these themes than together, in community? With help from one another, we can consider how Jesus' teachings call us to reorient our lives around God's salvific plan.

SEEK FIRST THE KINGDOM

In this section, your group will discuss questions related to the teaching in the video, the Scripture reading, and the week's daily devotionals. Perhaps the greatest theme of Luke's Gospel is Jesus' insistence that the kingdom of God is here, and it is has arrived through him. As Jesus makes his way to Jerusalem, he lays out God's new order for the world and how the people of God can put it into practice. While Jesus' destination is the fulfillment of God's purposes, it is by following his footsteps along the way that we learn the way of discipleship—The Disciple's Way. Jesus makes it clear that we have one main job: To seek first the kingdom of God. We do not waste our time judging who is in or who is out, trying to perfect our image, or worrying; neither are we to spend our energy hoarding, protecting, and clinging to our possessions. Through these questions, your group will dig deep into what it means to live in and for the kingdom of God, here and now, as a disciple of Jesus.

PRAYER REQUESTS

After the group discussion, you have the option of asking members for any prayer requests they'd like the group to pray for. There is a Prayer & Praise Journal included in this Study Guide to keep track of prayer requests and God's gracious answers!

CLOSING PRAYER

Close your group's time in prayer, either with someone leading in a spontaneous prayer, using the suggested prayer, or both. Be sure to finish your small group on time.

Week One

BLESSED EYES

Do you see the people of the world with the eyes of Jesus?

KEY VERSE

And he said to all, "If anyone would come after me, let him deny himself and take up his cross daily and follow me. For whoever would save his life will lose it, but whoever loses his life for my sake will save it. For what does it profit a man if he gains the whole world and loses or forfeits himself? For whoever is ashamed of me and of my words, of him will the Son of Man be ashamed when he comes in his glory and the glory of the Father and of the holy angels. But I tell you truly, there are some standing here who will not taste death until they see the kingdom of God."

LUKE 9:23-27

SESSION INTRODUCTION

Jesus taught his disciples that he must go to Jerusalem, suffer, die, and three days later rise from the dead. This fixed and focused intention sets the direction of the travel narrative and the disciples' journey. Jesus would teach that not only is this his intention—to go to the Cross—but it marks the direction of any and all who would follow him. The call is to "take up" our cross daily and follow Jesus.

As we set our eyes to the Cross, we gain an entirely new way of seeing the world and the people in it. Our eyes open to the larger vocation of being a disciple and we see the mission and plan of God revealed before us. The kingdom of God is visible to our eyes as we focus on the Cross. Worldly ways of looking at the world give way to kingdom eyesight.

With this new kingdom eyesight, our prejudiced categories for defining others according to worldly patterns give way to new definitions and new opportunities for mission. We see others as the precious souls they are, loved and sought by God. As our eyes open wider, we also become aware of the evil spiritual forces at work in this world to thwart God's purposes—and their fate. We see everything with the eyes of Jesus.

OPENING PRAYER

O God of all the nations of the earth: Remember the multitudes who have been created in your image but have not known the redeeming work of our Savior Jesus Christ; and grant that, by the prayers and labors of your holy Church, they may be brought to know and worship you as you have been revealed in your Son; who lives and reigns with you and the Holy Spirit, one God, for ever and ever. Amen. (BCP, P. 257)

GETTING STARTED

Take a moment to introduce yourselves. Answer the question: What are your hopes for this group?

Jesus says, "All who want to come after me must say no to themselves, take up their cross daily, and follow me." What do you think he means by this?

WATCH THE VIDEO

Play the video for your group, making sure the volume is adequate for all to hear and every member can see the video from where they're sitting. Use The Disciple's Way DVD or view with online streaming at www.sjd.org/disciplesway/.

STUDY NOTES

___

___

___

___

VIDEO NOTES

The disciple's sight includes:

> *Focused Eyes* – Following Jesus brings intention to your life. The disciple's face is set toward the Cross and Jesus' Resurrection. Have you taken up your cross and followed Jesus?

> *Missionary Eyes* – With focused intention comes a new purpose to reach the people of this world with the Good News of Jesus. The harvest is plentiful, but the workers are few. Do you see all the people of this world as the kingdom's harvest field?

> *Truthful Eyes* – The disciple sees the work of evil powers in this world operating to harm, discourage, and destroy.

> *Blessed Eyes* – The disciple also sees the fate of evil with the coming of Jesus. The path to victory is the Cross. The disciple sees the joy that is set before him in the reign of the risen Lord Jesus over all Creation.

From the video teachings and testimonies, take a moment to debrief with questions like these:

- *What resonated with you most?*

- *What did hear that was a new to you or hard to understand?*

- *What inspired you?*

Hear God's Word

Read Luke 10:25-37

TAKE THESE WORDS TO HEART

1. Why do you think the lawyer asked Jesus the question, "And who is my neighbor?" What do you think was behind his question?

2. In Jesus' story, three people "saw" the man left for dead on the road but were somehow unmoved. What was the problem with their "sight?"

3. What made the eyes of the Samaritan different?

4. In Jesus' Good Samaritan story, the neighbor is the one who gives mercy rather than the one who receives it. How does Jesus' way of telling the story provide a new perspective on the question of "Who is my neighbor?"

5. Is there anyone in your life who you have intentionally or unintentionally put outside the scope of "love your neighbor?"

SEEK FIRST THE KINGDOM

1. Jesus said, "No one who puts his hand to the plow and looks back is fit for the kingdom of God." (See Luke 9:57-62) What do you think this means? Do you ever struggle with "looking back" in this way?

2. As you think about the different types of eyes that make up a disciple's sight (focused eyes, missionary eyes, truthful eyes, blessed eyes), which set of eyes do you want to ask God to give you this week? Why?

3. Is there some mission field work the Lord has revealed to you that you'd like to take a step of faith towards fulfilling this week? Are you open to sharing this with the group?

PRAYER REQUESTS

You may want to share prayer requests with one another. There is a Prayer & Praise Journal found on p. 203 where you can keep track of your group's requests. Have someone close in prayer or pray the following prayer together:

CLOSING PRAYER

Open wide the eyes of my soul that I may see good in all things; Grant me this week some new vision of thy truth; Inspire me with the spirit of joy and gladness; and make me the cup of strength to suffering souls; in the name of the strong Deliverer, our only Lord and Savior, Jesus Christ. Amen. – Phillips Brooks, Forward Day by Day, Feb-Apr 2014

Week Two

TRUE HEART

Do you have a true heart for the Lord and a deep desire for his Spirit to transform you?

KEY VERSE

And I tell you, ask, and it will be given to you; seek, and you will find; knock, and it will be opened to you. For everyone who asks receives, and the one who seeks finds, and to the one who knocks it will be opened. What father among you, if his son asks for a fish, will instead of a fish give him a serpent; or if he asks for an egg, will give him a scorpion? If you then, who are evil, know how to give good gifts to your children, how much more will the heavenly Father give the Holy Spirit to those who ask him!

LUKE 11:9-13

SESSION INTRODUCTION

Being religious is not necessarily the same as being a true disciple. Jesus' strongest critique was directed at the religious hypocrisy of the Pharisees and scribes. Indeed, one of the most common complaints the unbelieving world levels at Christians and the Church is hypocrisy. We have all encountered people who "talk the talk" but do not "walk the walk."

If we are honest, being an authentic and genuine disciple of Jesus is hard. Genuine love and true holiness of life are Christian ideals that require deep inner transformation. We do not have the power to live as authentic disciples of Jesus, manifesting a true heart for God, alone.

Jesus calls us to the ideal as his disciples, but not without help. The gift of the Holy Spirit is the enlivening power behind the scenes of the authentic Christian life. The true heart of any believer is a Spirit-filled heart.

OPENING PRAYER

Almighty and most merciful God, grant that by the indwelling of your Holy Spirit we may be enlightened and strengthened for your service; through Jesus Christ our Lord, who lives and reigns with you, in the unity of the Holy Spirit, one God, now and for ever. Amen. (BCP, P. 251)

GETTING STARTED

How do you define the term "hypocrite?"

Why do you think hypocrisy is so destructive?

WATCH THE VIDEO

Play the video for your group, making sure the volume is adequate for all to hear and every member can see the video from where they're sitting. Use The Disciple's Way DVD or view with online streaming at www.sjd.org/disciplesway/.

STUDY NOTES

_____

_____

_____

_____

VIDEO NOTES

Jesus called the Pharisees and scribes "hypocrites." The term originally comes from the Greek theater and means "actor."

An authentic life is one in which the internal life (what God sees) and the external life (what people see) are genuinely aligned.

The antidote to hypocrisy is a vibrant life filled with the Holy Spirit of God. Jesus describes the Holy Spirit as a loving gift that God the Father wants to give to his children. Do you have any barriers to asking for the Holy Spirit?

From the video teachings and testimonies, take a moment to debrief with questions like these:

- *What resonated with you most?*

- *What did hear that was a new to you or hard to understand?*

- *What inspired you?*

Hear God's Word

Read Luke 11:17-28

TAKE THESE WORDS TO HEART

1. Jesus teaches that the evil spirit not only returns to the clean-swept home but brings friends with him. What else is needed in addition to a "clean and orderly" house to keep evil from taking up residence in us?

2. What are examples of evidence of the Holy Spirit dwelling in someone?

3. Jesus says, "Beware of the leaven of the Pharisees, which is hypocrisy" (Luke 12:1b). How do you define hypocrisy?

SEEK FIRST THE KINGDOM

1. Much like Israel, we often try to clean up our mess by ourselves and are surprised when our "demons" return seven-fold. What is something that you need to stop trying to fix on your own, and surrender to the Holy Spirit?

2. According to Jesus, it is not our familial roles or ancestry that give us privilege and blessing; rather, blessed are "those who hear the word of God and keep it!" (11:28) Is this truth liberating to you or unsettling? Why?

3. It is one thing to hear and *agree*, it is another thing to hear and *obey*. It is faithful obedience Jesus calls us to. Is there anything God has laid on your heart that you know to be true but are struggling to act upon?

4. Take some time to think together as a small group about what you could do as a group or church community to put your faith into action.

PRAYER REQUESTS

You may want to share prayer requests with one another. There is a Prayer & Praise Journal found on p. 203 where you can keep track of your group's requests. Have someone close in prayer or pray the following prayer together:

CLOSING PRAYER

Almighty and everlasting God, whose will it is to restore all things in your well-beloved Son, the King of kings and Lord of lords: Mercifully grant that the peoples of the earth, divided and enslaved by sin, may be freed and brought together under his most gracious rule; who lives and reigns with you and the Holy Spirit, one God, now and for ever. Amen. (BCP, P. 254)

Week Three

REALISTIC FAITH

Is your faith anchored in the unseen reality of God's kingdom or in the fleeting here-and-now?

KEY VERSE

There were some present at that very time who told him about the Galileans whose blood Pilate had mingled with their sacrifices. And he answered them, "Do you think that these Galileans were worse sinners than all the other Galileans, because they suffered in this way? No, I tell you; but unless you repent, you will all likewise perish. Or those eighteen on whom the tower in Siloam fell and killed them: do you think that they were worse offenders than all the others who lived in Jerusalem? No, I tell you; but unless you repent, you will all likewise perish."

LUKE 13:1-5

SESSION INTRODUCTION

The question of "why do bad things happen to good people?" is as old as the Garden of Eden. Our minds try to connect dots that cannot be connected and give reasons for the irrational. Evil makes no good sense.

Jesus encouraged his disciples to come to a realistic understanding of this world as one that has been corrupted by the fall of humanity into sin and is ultimately destined for judgment. This world is not where the disciple of Jesus puts their trust or faith. It is not the way things are supposed to be. This world is fallen, broken, and overrun by evil.

The disciple has a realistic faith that sees the unseen reality of the coming kingdom of God. Justice is coming, but it will be a slow process. The disciple must first endure a cross before resurrection breaks forth. This world must undergo judgement before the new heavens and new earth spring forth.

OPENING PRAYER

Grant us, Lord, not to be anxious about earthly things, but to love things heavenly; and even now, while we are placed among things that are passing away, to hold fast to those that shall endure; through Jesus Christ our Lord, who lives and reigns with you and the Holy Spirit, one God, for ever and ever. Amen. (BCP, P. 234)

GETTING STARTED

Do you ever feel that there must be more to life than this?

Why do you think people put so much trust in the kingdoms of this world rather than the kingdom of God?

WATCH THE VIDEO

Play the video for your group, making sure the volume is adequate for all to hear and every member can see the video from where they're sitting. Use The Disciple's Way DVD or view with online streaming at www.sjd.org/disciplesway/.

STUDY NOTES

_____

_____

_____

_____

VIDEO NOTES

Judgments – Jesus teaches his disciples concerning three coming judgements: Jesus on the Cross (33 AD), Jerusalem and Israel (70 AD), the world (unknown time).

Delay – The kingdom of God will come slowly and progressively, like a mustard seed that grows gradually into a tree or yeast that slowly works its way through dough. The delay of final judgement gives us and the people of this world precious time and opportunity to turn our lives over to God. In the meantime, we sometimes suffer as we prepare and wait for the great salvation.

Salvation – Ultimately, we need rescue from this world, evil, death, and corruption. Our salvation from the last judgement will come through faith in the first judgement, the Cross. Jesus calls this path of salvation the "narrow way."

From the video teachings and testimonies, take a moment to debrief with questions like these:

- *What resonated with you most?*

- *What did hear that was a new to you or hard to understand?*

- *What inspired you?*

Hear God's Word

Read Luke 13:18-30

TAKE THESE WORDS TO HEART

1. Do you recognize that this world is not your provision?

2. What is God's kingdom like compared to the kingdom of this world?

3. Someone from the crowd asks, "Lord, will those who are saved be few?" Who is assumed to be saved and who is not? What would these individuals need saving from? How does Jesus address this question?

SEEK FIRST THE KINGDOM

1. What could it look like to respond to Jesus' instruction to "Strive to enter through the narrow door?" (13:24)

2. How will our actions today effect the next generation of the Church? How are you participating in God's plan to restore all things?

3. On the way to Jerusalem, Jesus challenges people he meets to orient themselves around the priorities of the kingdom of God. This reorientation of life is the epitome of repentance and preparation. How has following the ways of Jesus caused you to reorient your life?

PRAYER REQUESTS

You may want to share prayer requests with one another. There is a Prayer & Praise Journal found on p. 203 where you can keep track of your group's requests. Have someone close in prayer or pray the following prayer together:

CLOSING PRAYER

Almighty God, whose beloved Son willingly endured the agony and shame of the cross for our redemption: Give us courage to take up our cross and follow him; who lives and reigns with you and the Holy Spirit, one God, now and for ever. Amen. (BCP, P. 252)

Week Four

ETERNAL FELLOWSHIP

> Are you seeking friendships that will bring you earthly advantage or eternal treasure?

KEY VERSE

He said also to the man who had invited him, "When you give a dinner or a banquet, do not invite your friends or your brothers or your relatives or rich neighbors, lest they also invite you in return and you be repaid. But when you give a feast, invite the poor, the crippled, the lame, the blind, and you will be blessed, because they cannot repay you. For you will be repaid at the resurrection of the just."

LUKE 14:12-14

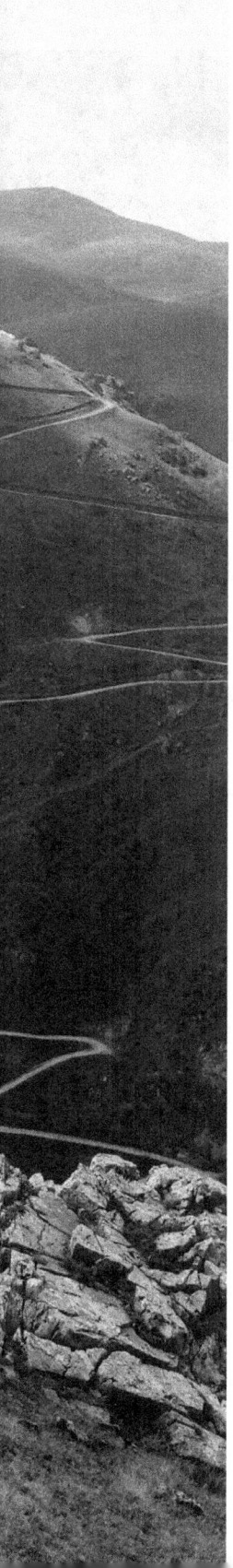

SESSION INTRODUCTION

"The greatest disease in the West today is not TB or leprosy; it is being unwanted, unloved, and uncared for. We can cure physical diseases with medicine, but the only cure for loneliness, despair, and hopelessness is love. There are many in the world who are dying for a piece of bread but there are many more dying for a little love. The poverty in the West is a different kind of poverty—it is not only a poverty of loneliness but also of spirituality. There's a hunger for love, as there is a hunger for God."[24] —Mother Teresa

The disciple of Jesus cultivates an eternal fellowship. The word fellowship comes from the Greek *koinonia*. It is used in the Bible to describe the deep Christian friendships that fellow believers share with one another; but the word also describes our communion with God through Christ. Out of this deep fellowship with God arise the most unusual relationships that cross typical human boundaries based on socio-economics, political parties, race, ethnicity, age, etc. Believers are one in Christ Jesus.

---

24. Mother Teresa, *A Simple Path* (New York: Ballantine Books, 1995), p. 79.

OPENING PRAYER

Grant, O merciful God, that your Church, being gathered together in unity by your Holy Spirit, may show forth your power among all peoples, to the glory of your Name; through Jesus Christ our Lord, who lives and reigns with you and the Holy Spirit, one God, for ever and ever. Amen. (BCP, P. 232)

GETTING STARTED

Do you enjoy having people over to your home? What are occasions or events you celebrate in your house?

What has been your most unlikely friendship?

WATCH THE VIDEO

Play the video for your group, making sure the volume is adequate for all to hear and every member can see the video from where they're sitting. Use The Disciple's Way DVD or view with online streaming at www.sjd.org/disciplesway/.

STUDY NOTES

_____
_____
_____
_____

VIDEO NOTES

Jesus' love for the amazingly varied types of people in this world translates into the most diverse organization on the planet: The Church. It is a global fellowship made up of every tongue, every tribe, every nation, and every people group on earth. Yet sometimes, in our individual congregations, our friendships are characterized more by worldly orderings than the eternal friendships that Jesus would see manifested among his people.

The Banquet – Jesus often describes Christian fellowship as a great banquet, like a wedding feast or a wealthy person's party. How does the eternal banquet compare to our earthly ones?

Koinonia – Fellow believers in Jesus share a deep bond with one another. This word also describes our communion with God through Christ.

Earthly Advantage – Many personal relationships are based on practical earthly connections—our business associations and typical circles where we do life. These are of benefit to us.

Eternal Treasure – Jesus encourages his disciples to put greater value on friends and relationships that will last for eternity. Some of these may be in our typical spheres of life, but they may also include some unlikely friendships.

Think about your closest friends. Do you share the same religious or political beliefs? How about ethnicity and culture? What about socioeconomic status? Share why there is or is not much diversity among those you spend the most time.

From the video teachings and testimonies, take a moment to debrief with questions like these:

- *What resonated with you most?*

- *What did hear that was a new to you or hard to understand?*

- *What inspired you?*

Hear God's Word

Read Luke 15:1-32

TAKE THESE WORDS TO HEART

1. Have you ever had an experience like the younger son where you "came to your senses" (v.17) and had to repair a broken relationship? Who "welcomed you back" into their life? What was the hardest part of that experience?

2. What about with God? If you have ever experienced a time of distance from God, what was your motivation for coming back to him?

3. Why do you think the Pharisees needed to hear these parables? What was Jesus trying to teach them?

4. What barriers have you experienced in your relationships that have kept you from receiving others in forgiveness and love as the father in the story did?

SEEK FIRST THE KINGDOM

1. Is there a younger prodigal brother in your life that needs to be welcomed back to the fellowship? How can the group pray for them?

2. Thinking about the various spheres of your life, is there a person you would not normally associate with that you might be willing to build an eternal friendship in Christ with? Who comes to your mind and heart?

PRAYER REQUESTS

You may want to share prayer requests with one another. There's a Prayer & Praise Journal found on p. 203 where you can keep track of your group's requests. Have someone close in prayer or pray the following prayer together:

CLOSING PRAYER

O God, who wonderfully created, and yet more wonderfully restored, the dignity of human nature: Grant that we may share the divine life of him who humbled himself to share our humanity, your Son Jesus Christ; who lives and reigns with you, in the unity of the Holy Spirit, one God, for ever and ever. Amen. (BCP, P. 252)

Week Five

GENEROUS SERVICE

Will you steward the blessings God has given you with grateful generosity?

KEY VERSE

One who is faithful in a very little is also faithful in much, and one who is dishonest in a very little is also dishonest in much. If then you have not been faithful in the unrighteous wealth, who will entrust to you the true riches? And if you have not been faithful in that which is another's, who will give you that which is your own? No servant can serve two masters, for either he will hate the one and love the other, or he will be devoted to the one and despise the other. You cannot serve God and money.

LUKE 16:10-13

SESSION INTRODUCTION

Jesus calls the finances and economy of this world "unrighteous wealth." No matter how holy and good we are, because of sin, all our human financial interactions have an element of worldly corruption. Yet Jesus encourages us to be in the world, yet not of the world.

The disciple of Jesus is encouraged to use "unrighteous wealth" in the generous service of the kingdom. We do this by serving God first and foremost and, by extension, using our money and possessions in the service of the kingdom.

Our attitude toward the things of this world becomes one of being *entrusted with them*, rather than *entitled to them*. It is a question of faithfulness. As Jesus puts it, "One who is faithful in very little is also faithful in much." Small actions of generosity translate into huge benefits for the kingdom and spiritual blessings for the giver.

OPENING PRAYER

O merciful Creator, your hand is open wide to satisfy the needs of every living creature: Make us always thankful for your loving providence; and grant that we, remembering the account that we must one day give, may be faithful stewards of your good gifts; through Jesus Christ our Lord, who with you and the Holy Spirit lives and reigns, one God, for ever and ever. Amen. (BCP, P. 259)

GETTING STARTED

If you had a million dollars to be given away to any charity, what would you give to?

Have you ever worked for two bosses (two masters) or supervised someone who reported to both you and other people? What was it like to balance competing priorities or different sets of expectations?

WATCH THE VIDEO

Play the video for your group, making sure the volume is adequate for all to hear and every member can see the video from where they're sitting. Use The Disciple's Way DVD or view with online streaming at www.sjd.org/disciplesway/.

STUDY NOTES

VIDEO NOTES

On Serving Two Masters – People can have a personal relationship to money, surrendered to it, as they properly should have to God instead. Jesus taught that it is not possible to serve two masters. One must take primacy. So for you, which is it: God or money?

Unrighteous Wealth – These are the resources of this world. The financial and economic systems of this world all share an element of corruption. Jesus says to use this for good.

True Riches – This is the capital of the kingdom of God. This is the investment we put into God's work and his people.

From the video teachings and testimonies, take a moment to debrief with questions like these:

- *What resonated with you most?*

- *What did hear that was a new to you or hard to understand?*

- *What inspired you?*

Hear God's Word

Read Luke 16:14-31

TAKE THESE WORDS TO HEART

1. How are "the rich man" and Lazarus described? Think about their clothes, their daily routines, their residences, and their actions in the story?

2. What can we learn from each of these characters?

3. What would you say was the rich man's sin?

SEEK FIRST THE KINGDOM

1. Why do you think Jesus spoke so much about love of money versus generosity? How have his teachings informed your relationship to money?

2. Who in your life do you think goes unnoticed? How can you be more intentional to see or give attention to those individuals that you overlook?

3. In most cultures, charitable giving is seen as honorable; so what keeps us from giving generously? How do we determine how much we need and what we can afford to share with others?

4. Whose job is it to care for the poor? Feed the hungry? House the homeless? Clothe the naked? Etc.?

PRAYER REQUESTS

You may want to share prayer requests with one another. There's a Prayer & Praise Journal found on p. 203 where you can keep track of your group's requests. Have someone close in prayer or pray the following prayer together:

CLOSING PRAYER

Lord, make us instruments of your peace. Where there is hatred, let us sow love; where there is injury, pardon; where there is discord, union; where there is doubt, faith; where there is despair, hope; where there is darkness, light; where there is sadness, joy. Grant that we may not so much seek to be consoled as to console; to be understood as to understand; to be loved as to love. For it is in giving that we receive; it is in pardoning that we are pardoned; and it is in dying that we are born to eternal life. Amen. —A Prayer attributed to St. Francis (BCP, P. 833)

Week Six

SELFLESS HUMILITY

Do you find your value in comparison to others or in humble embrace of God's mercy?

KEY VERSE

And will not God give justice to his elect, who cry to him day and night? Will he delay long over them? I tell you; he will give justice to them speedily. Nevertheless, when the Son of Man comes, will he find faith on earth?

SESSION INTRODUCTION

Pride keeps us from taking the risks required for God's mission. Our ego gets in the way. Having a faith like the children that ran to Jesus, The Disciple's Way requires vulnerability and a selfless humility.

There are many barriers that prevent us from truly following Jesus with all of our heart, mind, soul, and strength. The two biggest are self-protection and fear of others. Self-protection prevents us from having a realistic view of self and God. Paradoxically, when we are willing to lose our self for God, we are in the safest place—we gain our life.

Far too often, we judge ourselves by our horizontal relations to others around us. The comparison game keeps us stuck in either self-righteousness or prideful insecurity. Worth, value, and significance are derived from our vertical relationship to God. When we have nothing to lose in this world, we have the kingdom of God to gain.

OPENING PRAYER

Grant us, O Lord, to trust in you with all our hearts; for, as you always resist the proud who confide in their own strength, so you never forsake those who make their boast of your mercy; through Jesus Christ our Lord, who lives and reigns with you and the Holy Spirit, one God, now and for ever. Amen. (BCP, P. 233)

GETTING STARTED

Have you ever had a person of high status or power in the world treat you with unexpected kindness or humility? What was that like?

When you play the "comparison game" with others, what types of measures do you tend to use? Wealth, physical attractiveness, athletic skill, personality, position, etc.?

WATCH THE VIDEO

Play the video for your group, making sure the volume is adequate for all to hear and every member can see the video from where they're sitting. Use The Disciple's Way DVD or view with online streaming at www.sjd.org/disciplesway/.

STUDY NOTES

_____

_____

_____

VIDEO NOTES

Impossible! – In and of ourselves, we have no power to save ourselves. Jesus described it like trying to thread a camel through the eye of a needle. But God has made a way.

The Way of the Cross – Ultimately The Disciple's Way is Jesus' way. It leads to a cross, and that requires a daily dying to self.

Seeking Jesus – Like Zacchaeus, who was short in stature, our call is to seek Jesus' way relentlessly, against all obstacles. In seeking, we are found.

One Mina – We all have one life to live and give for God. How will you invest yours for the kingdom?

In the teaching video, the comparison was made between the rich young ruler and Zacchaeus. After Jesus describes how difficult it is for a rich person to enter the kingdom of God, the disciples ask, "Who then can be saved?" What sets Zacchaeus apart from the rich young ruler?

From the video teachings and testimonies, take a moment to debrief with questions like these:

- *What resonated with you most?*

- *What did hear that was a new to you or hard to understand?*

- *What inspired you?*

Hear God's Word

Read Luke 18:9-14

TAKE THESE WORDS TO HEART

1. What did you just hear the Word say to you?

2. Contrast the two characters in the parable. How are they similar? How are they different? Which of these characters do you identify with? How so?

3. What is the standard by which the Pharisee is measuring himself? What is the standard by which the tax collector is measuring himself?

4. Where have you seen judgement of others manifest in your own life? Is there anyone you "look on" with disgust, contempt, or pity?

SEEK FIRST THE KINGDOM

1. Do you feel like it is possible to live an honorable, faithful life on your own merit? Explain your experience with this.

2. Have you ever caught yourself saying a "Thank God I'm not like…" prayer? Is that a bad prayer?

3. How have you learned to rely on God instead of yourself?

4. What are some ways you will practice "picking up your cross and dying daily" for Jesus?

5. The video talked about how we have "one mina," one life to invest for the kingdom. From this study of Luke's travel narrative, do you think you will be intentionally living differently in any way? How so?

PRAYER REQUESTS

You may want to share prayer requests with one another. There is a Prayer & Praise Journal found on p. 203 where you can keep track of your group's requests. Have someone close in prayer or pray the following prayer together:

CLOSE IN PRAYER

Almighty God, whose beloved Son willingly endured the agony and shame of the cross for our redemption: Give us courage to take up our cross and follow him; who lives and reigns with you and the Holy Spirit, one God, now and for ever. Amen. (BCP, P. 252)

Appendices

FREQUENTLY ASKED QUESTIONS

What do we do on the first night of our group?

Have a party! A "get to know you" coffee, dinner, or dessert is a great way to launch a new study. You may want to review the Small Group Covenant (page 200) and share the names of a few friends you can invite to join you. But most importantly, have fun before your study time begins.

How long will this group meet?

Most groups meet weekly for at least their first six weeks, but every other week can work as well. We strongly recommend that the group meet for the first six months on a weekly basis if at all possible. This allows for continuity and, if people miss a meeting, they aren't gone for a whole month.

At the end of this study, each group member may decide if he or she wants to continue on for another six-week study. Some groups launch relationships for years to come, and others are stepping-stones into another group experience. Either way, enjoy the journey.

Can we do this study on our own?

Absolutely! This may sound crazy, but one of the best ways to do this study is not with a full house but with a few friends. You may choose to gather with another couple who would enjoy some relational time (perhaps going to the movies or having a quiet dinner) and then walking through this six-week study. Jesus will be with you even if there are only two of you (Matthew 18:20).

Where do we find new members for our group?

Finding members can be troubling, especially for new groups that have only a few people or for existing groups that lose a few people along the way. We encourage you to pray with your group and then brainstorm a list of people from work, church, your neighborhood, your children's school, family, the gym, and so forth. Use the five circles to identify potential group members with whom you would like to build a spiritual friendship. Have each group member invite several of the people on his or her list.

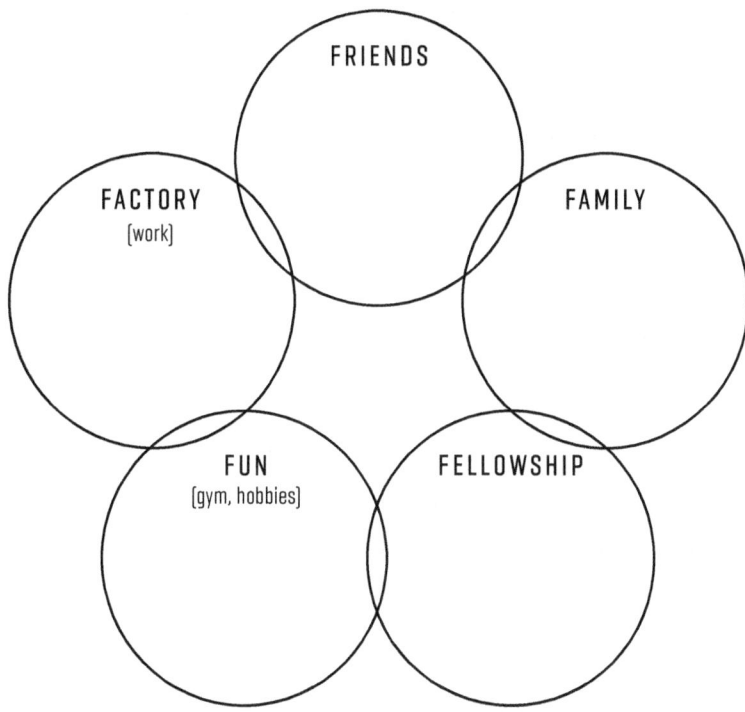

No matter how you find members, it's vital that you stay on the lookout for new people to join your group. All groups tend to go through healthy attrition—the result of moves, sending out new leaders, ministry opportunities, and so forth—and if the group gets too small, it could be at risk of ending. If you and your group stay open to ideas, you'll be amazed at the people God sends your way. The next person just might become a friend for life. You never know!

What if this group is not working for us?

You are not alone! This could be the result of a personality conflict, life stage difference, geographical distance, level of spiritual maturity, or any number of things. Relax. Pray for God's direction, and at the end of this six-week study, decide whether to continue with this group or find another. You don't typically buy the first car you test drive or marry the first person you date, and the same goes with a group. However, don't bail out before the six weeks are up— God might have something to teach you. Also, don't run from conflict or prejudge people before you have given them a chance. God is still working in your life, too!

Who is the leader?

Most groups have an official leader. But ideally, the group will mature and members will rotate the leadership of meetings. We have discovered that healthy groups rotate hosts/leaders and homes on a regular basis. This model ensures that all members grow, make their unique contribution, and develop their gifts. This study guide and the Holy Spirit can keep things on track even when you rotate leaders. Christ has promised to be in your midst as you gather. Ultimately, God is your leader each step of the way.

How do we handle the childcare needs in our group?

Very carefully. This can be a sensitive issue. We suggest that you empower the group to openly brainstorm solutions. You may try one option that works for a while and then adjust over time. Our favorite approach is for adults to meet in the living room or dining room and to share the cost of a babysitter (or two) who can watch the children in a different part of the house. This way, parents don't have to be away from their children all evening when their children are too young to be left at home. A second option is to use one home for the children and a second home (close by or a phone call away) for the adults. A third idea is to rotate the responsibility of providing a lesson or care for the children either in the same home or in another home nearby. This can be an incredible blessing for young ones. Finally, the most common solution is to decide that you need to have a night to invest in your spiritual lives individually or as a couple and to make your own arrangements for childcare. No matter what decision the group makes, the best approach is to dialogue openly about both the need and the solution.

Small Group Covenant

OUR PURPOSE

To provide a predictable environment where participants experience authentic Christian community to grow spiritually.

GROUP ATTENDANCE

To give priority to the group meeting. We will call or email if we will be late or absent. (Completing the Group Calendar on page 202 will minimize this issue.)

SAFE ENVIRONMENT

To help create a safe place where people can be heard and feel loved. (Please, no quick answers, snap judgments, or simple fixes.)

RESPECT DIFFERENCES

To be gentle and gracious with different spiritual maturity levels, personal opinions, temperaments, or "imperfections" in fellow group members. We are all works in progress.

CONFIDENTIALITY

To keep anything that is shared strictly confidential and within the group, and to avoid sharing improper information about those outside the group.

ENCOURAGEMENT FOR GROWTH

To be not just takers, but givers of life. We want to spiritually multiply our lives by serving others with our God-given gifts.

SHARED OWNERSHIP

To remember that every member is a minister and to ensure that each attender will share a small team role or responsibility over time.

ROTATING HOSTS, FACILITATORS, AND HOMES

To encourage different people to host the group in their homes and to rotate the responsibility of facilitating each meeting. (See the Group Calendar on page 202.)

Group Calendar

Planning and calendaring can help ensure the greatest participation at every meeting. At the end of each meeting, review this calendar. Be sure to include a regular rotation of host homes and facilitators, and don't forget birthdays, socials, church events, holidays, and mission/ministry projects.

FACILITATOR	SNACKS	HOST HOME	SESSION	DATE
			1	
			2	
			3	
			4	
			5	
			6	

Prayer & Praise Journal

SESSION 1 ————————————————

SESSION 2 ————————————————

SESSION 3 ————————————————

SESSION 4 ————————————————

SESSION 5 ————————————————

SESSION 6 ————————————————

Small Group Roster

Use the chart below to collect names and contact information from all of the group members. We suggest that one member (other than the host) "own" the task of collecting and distributing the contact information to everyone—via group text message or email—so that people can be in touch.

NAME	EMAIL	PHONE

Small Group Leader Helps

HOSTING AN OPEN HOUSE

If you're starting a new group, try planning an Open House before your first formal group meeting. Even if you have only two to four core members, it's a great way to break the ice and prayerfully consider who else might be open to joining you over the next few weeks. You can also use this kick-off meeting to hand out books, spend some time getting to know each other, discuss each person's expectations for the group, and briefly pray for each other. A simple meal or good dessert always make a kick-off meeting more fun. After people introduce themselves and share how they ended up being at the meeting (you can play a game to see who has the wildest story!), have everyone respond to a few icebreaker questions, such as:

- What is your favorite family vacation?

- What is one thing you love about your church/our community?

- What are two things about your life growing up that most people here don't know?

Next, ask everyone to tell what he or she hopes to get out of the study. You might want to review the Small Group Covenant in the Study Guide and talk about each person's expectations and priorities. Finally, set an open chair (maybe two) in the center of your group and explain that it represents someone who would enjoy or benefit from this group who isn't here yet.

Ask people to pray about inviting someone to join the group over the next few weeks. Hand out postcards and have everyone write an invitation or two. Don't worry about ending up with too many people; you can always have one discussion circle in the living room and another in the dining room after you watch the lesson. Each group could then report prayer requests and progress at the end of the session.

You can skip this kick-off meeting if your time is limited, but you'll experience a huge benefit if you take the time to connect with one another in this way.

LEADING FOR THE FIRST TIME

Seven common leadership experiences. Welcome to life out in front!

- Sweaty palms are a healthy sign. The Bible says God is gracious to the humble. Remember who is in control; the time to worry is when you're not worried. Those who are soft in heart (and sweaty palmed) are those whom God is sure to speak through.

- Seek support. Ask your leader, co-leader, or a close friend to pray for you and prepare with you before the session. Walking through the study will help you anticipate potentially difficult questions and discussion topics.

- Bring your uniqueness to the study. Lean into who you are and how God wants you to uniquely lead the study.

- Prepare. Prepare. Prepare. Go through the session, read the section of Scripture. If you are using the Video, listen to the teaching segment. Consider writing in a journal or praying through the day to prepare yourself for what God wants to do. Don't wait until the last minute to prepare.

- Ask for feedback so you can grow. Perhaps in an email or on index cards handed out at the study, have everyone write down three things you did well and one thing you could improve on. Don't get defensive. Instead, show an openness to learn and grow.

- Share with your group what God is doing in your heart. God is searching for those whose hearts are fully his. Share your trials and victories. We promise that people will relate.

- Prayerfully consider whom you would like to pass the baton to next week. It's only fair. God is ready for the next member of your group to go on the faith journey you just traveled. Make it fun and expect God to do the rest.

LEADERSHIP TRAINING 101

Congratulations! You have responded to the call to help shepherd Jesus' flock. There are few other tasks in the family of God that surpass the contribution you will be making. As you prepare to lead, whether it is one session or the entire series, here are a few thoughts to keep in mind. We encourage you to read these and review them with each new discussion leader before he or she leads.

1. Remember that you are not alone. God knows everything about you, and he knew that you would be asked to lead this group. Remember that it is common for all good leaders to feel that they are not ready to lead. Moses, Solomon, Jeremiah, and Timothy were all reluctant to lead. God promises, "Never will I leave you; never will I forsake you" (Hebrews 13:5). Whether you are leading for one evening, for several weeks, or for a lifetime, you will be blessed as you serve.

2. Don't try to do it alone. Pray right now for God to help you build a healthy leadership team. If you can enlist a co-leader to help you lead the group, you will find your experience to be much richer. This is your chance to involve as many people as you can in building a healthy group. All you have to do is call and ask people to help. You'll probably be surprised at the response.

3. Just be yourself. If you won't be you, who will? God wants you to use your unique gifts and temperament. Don't try to do things exactly like another leader; do them in a way that fits you! Just admit it when you don't have an answer and apologize when you make a mistake. Your group will love you for it, and you'll sleep better at night!

4. Prepare for your meeting ahead of time. Review the session and write down your responses to each question. Pay special attention to exercises that ask group members to do something other than engage in discussion, like take an action. These exercises will help your group live what the Bible teaches, not just talk about it.

5. Pray for your group members by name. Before you begin your session, go around the room in your mind and pray for each member. Ask God to use your time together to touch the heart of every person uniquely. Expect God to lead you to whomever he wants you to encourage or challenge in a special way. If you listen, God will surely lead!

6. When you ask a question, be patient. Someone will eventually respond. Sometimes people need a moment or two of silence to think about the question. Keep in mind, if silence doesn't bother you, it won't bother anyone else. After someone responds, affirm the response with a simple "thanks" or "good job." Then ask, "How about somebody else?" or "Would someone who hasn't shared like to add anything?" Be sensitive to new people or members who aren't ready to say, pray, or do anything. If you give them a safe setting, they will blossom over time.

7. Provide transitions between questions. When guiding the discussion, always read aloud the transitional paragraphs and the questions. Ask the group if anyone would like to read the paragraphs or Bible passages. Don't call on anyone, but ask for volunteers; then, be patient until someone begins. Be sure to thank the people who read aloud.

8. Break up into small groups each week or a larger group won't stay. If your group has a lot of people, we strongly encourage you to have the group gather sometimes in discussion circles of three or four people during the Take These Words to Heart or Seek First the Kingdom sections of the study. With a greater opportunity to talk in small circles, people will connect more with the study, apply more quickly what they're learning, and ultimately get more out of it. A small circle also encourages a quiet person to participate and tends to minimize the effect of a more dominant or vocal member. It can also help people feel more loved in your group.

    When you gather again at the end of the section, you can have one person summarize the highlights from each circle. Small circles are also helpful during prayer time. People who are not accustomed to praying aloud will feel more comfortable trying it with just two or three others.

    Also, prayer requests won't take as much time, so circles will have more time to actually pray. When you gather back with the whole group, you can have one person from each circle briefly update everyone on the prayer requests. People are more willing to break into small circles to pray if they know the whole group will hear all the prayer requests.

9. Rotate facilitators weekly. At the end of each meeting, ask the group who should lead the following week. Let the group help select your weekly facilitator. You may be perfectly capable of leading each time, but you will help others grow in their faith and gifts if you give them

opportunities to lead. You can use the Small Group Calendar to fill in the names of the different leaders for all the meetings if you prefer.

10. One final challenge (for new or first-time leaders): Before your first opportunity to lead, look up each of the five passages listed below. Read each one as a devotional exercise to help equip yourself with a shepherd's heart. Trust us on this one. If you do this, you will be more than ready to lead your first meeting.

MATTHEW 9:36

1 PETER 5:2-4

PSALM 23

EZEKIEL 34:11-16

1 THESSALONIANS 2:7-8, 11-12

www.ingramcontent.com/pod-product-compliance
Lightning Source LLC
Chambersburg PA
CBHW070056080526
44586CB00013B/1082